YOUNG SAINTS

PORTRAITS BY STÉPHANIE SON
COMICS BY TRISTAN GARNIER

Under the direction of Romain Lizé, President, Magnificat
Editor, Magnificat: Isabelle Galmiche
Editors, Ignatius: Vivian Dudro, Thomas Jacobi
Translator: Magnificat · Ignatius
Proofreader: Kathleen Hollenbeck
Layout Designers: Armelle Riva, Gauthier Delauné
Production: Thierry Dubus, Audrey Bord

Original French edition: *Enfants Saints*
© Mame, Paris, 2023
© 2024 by Magnificat, New York · Ignatius Press, San Francisco
All rights reserved
ISBN Magnificat 978-1-63967-070-3 · ISBN Ignatius Press 978-1-62164-714-0

Charlotte Grossetête

YOUNG SAINTS

Fifteen Extraordinary Lives from Blandina to Carlo Acutis

Magnificat • Ignatius

Contents

Saint Blandina (c. 162–177) 6

Saint Tarcisius (third century) 12

Saint Aloysius Gonzaga (1568–1591) 18

Saint Kateri Tekakwitha (1656–1680) 24

Saint Dominic Savio (1842–1857) 30

Blessed Pier Giorgio Frassati (1901–1925) 36

Saints Francisco and Jacinta Marto (1908–1919, 1910–1920) . . . 42

Venerable Anne de Guigné (1911–1922) 48

Saint José Luis Sánchez del Rio (1913–1928) 54

Blessed Marcel Callo (1921–1945) 60

Venerable Antonietta Meo (1930–1937) 66

Servant of God Claire de Castelbajac (1953–1975) 72

Blessed Sandra Sabattini (1961–1984) 78

Blessed Chiara Badano (1971–1990) 84

Blessed Carlo Acutis (1991–2006) 90

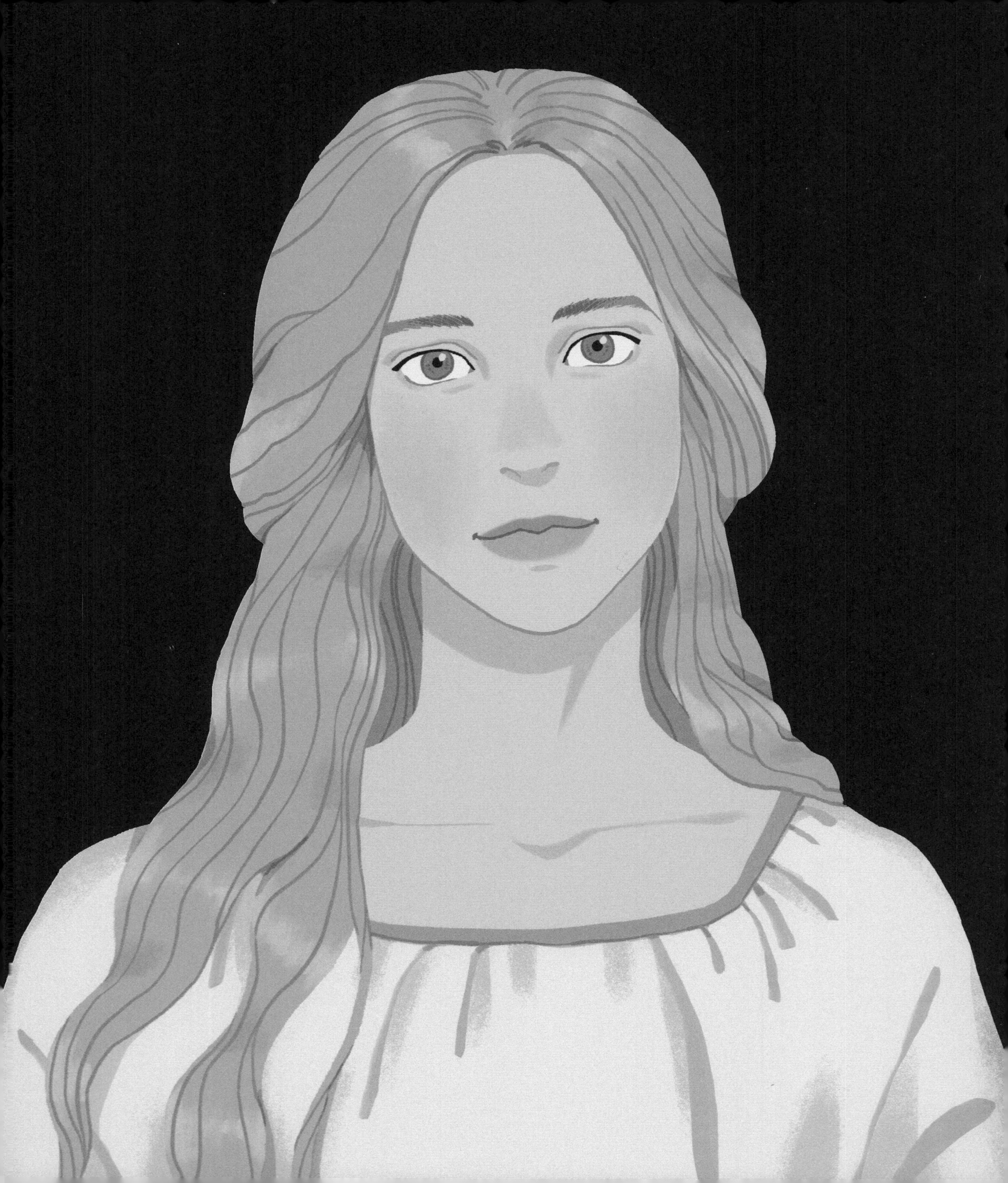

Saint Blandina

(c. 162–177)

Blandina was a young slave, whose life was of no importance in the unequal society of the Roman Empire. But she belonged to the newborn Christian Church, where there were no masters or slaves, only children of God. And these children of God were incredibly brave.

A Slave

Blandina came out of the house, two empty baskets in her hands. Such a beautiful day to go shopping for her mistress!

Lyon[1] was a rich city, and even at this early hour, the market was already buzzing with activity. Blandina, quiet and cheerful, liked the joyous uproar of the merchants and customers chatting loudly between stalls packed with merchandise and overflowing with fragrances. She wove her way through the crowd. No one paid attention to her, since her simple clothes revealed her status as a slave. People kept their eyes instead on the wealthy marketgoers in their fine dress. And yet, Blandina felt free, with an inner liberty that no one could steal from her.

The Secret of Freedom

"Hello, my little Blandina!" called out a familiar voice.

The young slave turned around, and her face lit up. The old man calling her was Bishop Pothinus, accompanied by Biblis, a woman from their community. They were coming to buy wine for the Lord's Supper—the Christian celebration that recalls the last meal Jesus Christ shared with his disciples.

"Are you coming tonight?" Pothinus asked.

"Yes, I am," Blandina answered with a radiant smile. "My mistress gives me the evening off."

---
1. Today in France. During the Roman Empire, the city was called Lugdunum.

This is the secret of Blandina's freedom. She belongs to a family of Christians, who consider all as children of the same Father. In their eyes, there are neither slaves nor masters, only the baptized, saved by Jesus Christ.

Market Gossip

"These Christians are suspect," a customer nearby said in a low voice, once Pothinus and his two companions had moved away.

The wine merchant turned to him, eyes widening. "And why is that?"

"Their meetings," the customer replied. "Terrible things happen there! They commit crimes that neither you nor I can even imagine."

The merchant stammered: "Do you—do you really think so? Christians seem like nice and honest people."

"Don't be fooled by appearances," the customer said. "They refuse to worship the emperor. Remember the floods this winter? That was their fault! They angered the goddess Cybele. And then," the customer added, even lower, "they eat human flesh!"

"We Are Christians, and We Have Done Nothing Wrong."

As time passed, rumors continued to spread. Before long, no one would risk defending Christians, so horrifying were the things said about them. One day, Roman authorities decided to put an end to their community. Blandina was arrested, along with fifty other Christians.

Bishop Pothinus died of exhaustion in prison. The others were tortured. To save her life, a terrified Biblis told her accusers that she no longer believed in Jesus. But then she remembered that life on the earth is nothing compared to the eternal life promised by Jesus. So, she cried in a loud voice: "That's not true! I am a Christian, and I'm proud and happy to be one!"

Despite the Romans' abuse, Blandina kept her cheer, repeating, "We are Christians, and we have done no wrong."

Her accusers grew angry. "That's a lie!" they exclaimed. "And for it, you will be put to death in the arena!"

But Blandina kept repeating the same words, in a clear voice: "We are Christians, and we have done nothing wrong."

Many witnesses were impressed. They knew that she was telling the truth. Later, despite the danger, some would dare to follow her example and ask to be baptized.

In the amphitheater of Lyon, a wild crowd was waiting with excitement in the sun.

Father, look at this girl! She is my age. She looks like me.

She's a slave. And a Christian. Nothing like you.

OOOOOH!

KILL HER!

LOOK AT THESE ANIMAL TRAITORS!

A slave, but she has the composure of a princess! What is the secret of her strength?

Some spectators were furious, yet others were amazed.

Boring!

Unbelievable! This girl is protected!

Blandina was eventually beheaded, but her martyrdom inspired many in Lyon to embrace her faith. The Church in Lyon was alive, and it continued to bear fruit.

BLANDINA, the Gentle Strength of Faith

First name: Blandina
Born: ca. 162, in what is now Lyon, France
Died: 177, in what is now Lyon, France
Occupation: Slave
Moments of weakness: Unknown
Moments of strength: Joy, moral courage, and confidence in front of her executioners
Patroness of: Young girls and the city of Lyon, France

Did You Know?

Christian artists represent Blandina as a serene young girl with a lion at her feet, to remind us that the animals in the amphitheater did not want to kill her. She also holds a palm in her hand. The palm is the symbol of the martyrs, in reference to the book of Revelation, where Saint John has a vision of a crowd of people dressed in white, holding palms in their hands and standing in front of the throne of the Lord. The angel explains to him that they are the ones "who have come out of the great tribulation" (Rev 7:14).

EUSEBIUS OF CAESAREA (ca. 265–339) Eusebius was bishop of the city of Caesarea, in Palestine. He survived the persecution of Diocletian and became close to Emperor Constantine I, who granted the freedom of worship to Christians in 313. Eusebius wrote the story of the early times of the Church and recalled the martyrdom of Saint Blandina in book 5 of his *Church History*.

Biblis

According to Eusebius of Caesarea, Biblis, another Christian martyr, momentarily renounced her faith (as Saint Peter did after the arrest of Jesus). A person who claims to renounce his religion under threat or torture is called a "renegade" or an "apostate." Eusebius added that Biblis recovered herself quickly.

---

43 B.C. Foundation of Lyon (called Lugdunum, in what is now France)

Birth of Jesus

A.D. 157 The Church of Lyon flourishes under Bishop Pothinus and his assistant, Irenaeus.

ca. A.D. 162 Birth of Blandina (precise date unknown)

A.D. 177 Martyrdom of Blandina, Pothinus, and many other Christians in Lyon

ca. A.D. 330 Eusebius of Caesarea publishes *Church History*, in which he recounts Blandina's story.

Prayer to Saint Blandina

Saint Blandina,
the Word of God set you free;
it was your strength and your joy;
it became your reason for living.
Help us to listen to God's Word,
to allow it to transform us
and bring us happiness.

Help us to live as disciples of Jesus,
proclaiming his love all around us.

May your radiant faith and your smile inspire us.

Watch over all Christians who, today,
are persecuted around the world
and need help from heaven to stand firm.
Amen.

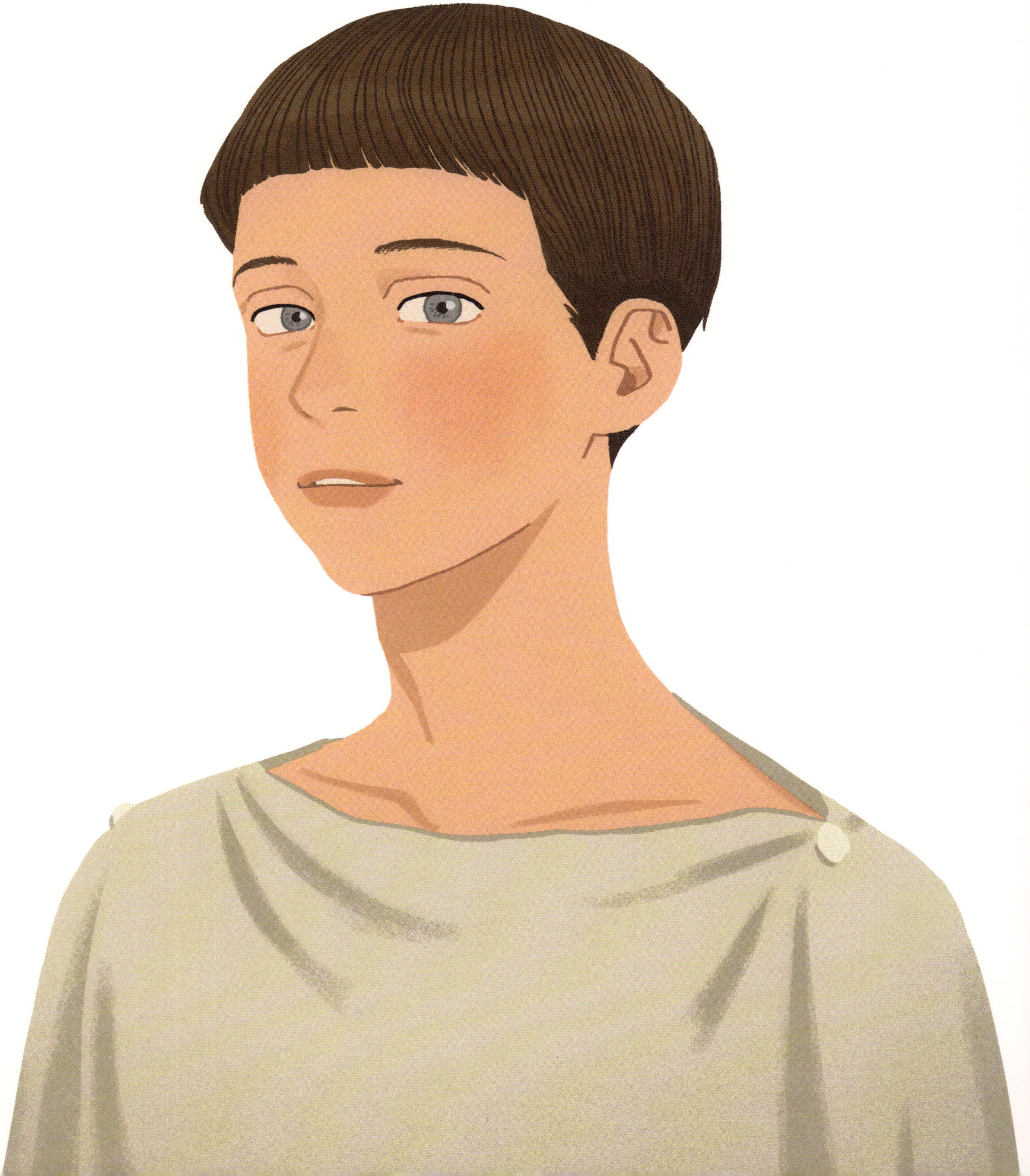

Saint Tarcisius
(third century)

Rome, A.D. 257. Emperor Valerian launched a vast persecution against Christians. Imperial soldiers arrested them without cause and confiscated their belongings, filling the empire's treasury. Many Christians languished in prison, and the ones who were still free lived in fear. Among these who lived under threat was the young altar server Tarcisius.

Danger in the Air

The celebration was over, but the Christians in the Catacombs of Saint Callixtus took their time finishing their silent prayer. No one was in a hurry to go back into the daylight. Over the past few months, Rome had become a dangerous city for Jesus Christ's followers. The number of arrests was growing, especially among Christians whose nobility and wealth were coveted by the emperor. Even the catacombs were not a safe refuge, since soldiers knew these underground tunnels well. Pope Stephen I had been put to death in there just a few weeks before, while he was celebrating Mass. Despite the risk, it was comforting to stay together to pray in these cool, dark galleries, the resting place of many fellow Christians who had already returned to God.

Important Mission

Suddenly, the voice of the priest broke the silence: "Who would like to go and give Communion to our brothers in prison? I have to visit Trophimus, who is sick at home."

A boy looked up. He was Tarcisius, the altar server. Under the light of the torch, he looked at the faces around him and saw that everyone was hesitating. Visits to the prisoners were allowed, but if you came across an unwilling guard, you risked finding yourself on the wrong side of the bars, or even thrown into the dungeon without a trial.

"I will go!" Tarcisius said.

"No, not you," the priest replied. "You are too young."

All eyes turned to him, and Tarcisius stood up straight. "Precisely," he said calmly. "My youth will offer the best shield for the Eucharist. I won't interest them. What could they confiscate from me?"

A Great Honor

The priest stifled a sigh. Tarcisius was right, alas! It was money that the emperor wanted above everything.

He wrapped in a white cloth the little piece of bread that had become the Body of Christ at the celebration of the Eucharist.

"Go and take Jesus to our brothers," he said quietly, handing the little package to Tarcisius.

The child hid the precious parcel under his tunic, pressed close to his heart. He was happy. He received the Eucharist as often as possible, but this was the first time that he had been entrusted with the honor of carrying God with him!

Then the priest added, "I don't need to tell you that you have to be extremely cautious."

Tarcisius smiled at him. He put the folds of his clothes back in place to hide the discreet bump of Jesus against his heart.

"I would rather be killed than let someone attack Jesus," he replied.

In Good Company

The priest made a final announcement: Tomorrow's assembly would take place at the home of Lawrence, a Christian who lived in another part of town. It was safer to change locations for each meeting.

The Christians left through the gallery to go back into the open air. Tarcisius and the priest came out last.

"Which route will you take to go to the prison?" the priest asked the young boy.

"Via Appia! It is the shortest path," Tarcisius answered.

"Avoid any encounters. I don't like advising you to be suspicious, but you will be alone, so—"

"Alone?" Tarcisius repeated with a little grin, pointing to the place where he was hiding Jesus. "I have never walked in such good company!"

On the Via Appia that crosses Rome...

These people seem to be waiting for me.

Lord, lead me toward safe roads, in spite of those I encounter on my way.

Oh, hello, Tarcisius.

In a hurry?

What are you hiding?

Let me go.

He is a Christian!

Death to all Christians!

"Even though I walk through the valley of the shadow of death, I fear no evil; for you are with me; your rod and your staff, they comfort me."*

*Psalm 23:4

Tarcisius gave his life to protect the Host. He is the patron saint of altar servers and First Communicants.

TARCISIUS, God's Brave Young Courier

Name: Tarcisius
Born: Third century, in Rome, Italy
Died: 257, in Rome, Italy
Occupation: Altar boy
Moments of weakness: Unknown
Moments of strength: Demonstrated great love for the Eucharist, died defending the Sacred Host
Patron of: Altar servers and children receiving their First Communion. His feast day is August 15.

Did You Know?

In the third century, the Catacombs of Saint Callixtus served as the official cemetery of the Church in Rome. Sixteen popes who died between the second and fourth centuries were among those buried there.

☞ **THE CATACOMBS OF SAINT CALLIXTUS** Located near the Via Appia and excavated around the middle of the second century, the Catacombs of Saint Callixtus are the largest in Rome. The complex has four underground levels and spans more than twelve miles. It is the oldest Christian cemetery in Rome. About a half million early Christians were laid to rest there, including Saint Tarcisius.

☞ **THE EPITAPH OF TARCISIUS** It was Pope Damasus I (305–384) who passed on the story of Tarcisius by having these lines inscribed on the young martyr's tomb: "The virtuous Tarcisius carried off the trophy from the enemy; when a crowd of wicked people urged him to show it to the impious, he preferred to lose his life and be killed rather than surrender the divine body to raging dogs."

What Were the Catacombs Used For?

Although they occasionally served as meeting places, the Christian catacombs were initially cemeteries (from the Latin *coemeteria*, or "dormitories," places where the dead awaited the resurrection). Unlike Romans, Christians refused to burn the bodies of the deceased. Thus, they had to bury them outside the city in accord with the law; the catacombs are located outside the walls of the ancient city.

Chronology of Persecutions against Christians in the Roman Empire

Ancient Christian sources refer to ten waves of persecutions of varying magnitude. Here are six of them:

A.D. 64 — Persecutions of Nero. Emperor Nero accuses the Christians of having set fire to the city of Rome. Saints Peter and Paul are executed.

A.D. 112 — Persecutions of Trajan. Christianity spreads and worries the authorities. The emperor allows Christians to be punished for causing public disorder.

A.D. 177 — Persecutions of Marcus Aurelius. Martyrdom of Saint Blandina and her companions.

A.D. 249–250 — Persecutions of Decius. The emperor imposes the obligation to make sacrifices to the Roman gods to protect the empire; Christians who refuse are put to death.

A.D. 257–258 — Persecutions of Valerian. Martyrdom of Tarcisius by stoning.

A.D. 303–304 — Persecutions of Diocletian, the most violent of all. Thousands of Christians—even members of the army and the imperial administration—are killed for disloyalty to the empire and its gods.

Prayer to Saint Tarcisius

Saint Tarcisius,
you were a friend of Jesus,
defending the Host
they wanted to take from you.

You knew that God was there,
sheltered by your hands.

Watch over us when we receive the Eucharist.
Help us to receive him with an ardent faith
so that we honor and love Jesus as he deserves,
as our Savior, teacher, and friend
who comes to dwell in us.
Amen.

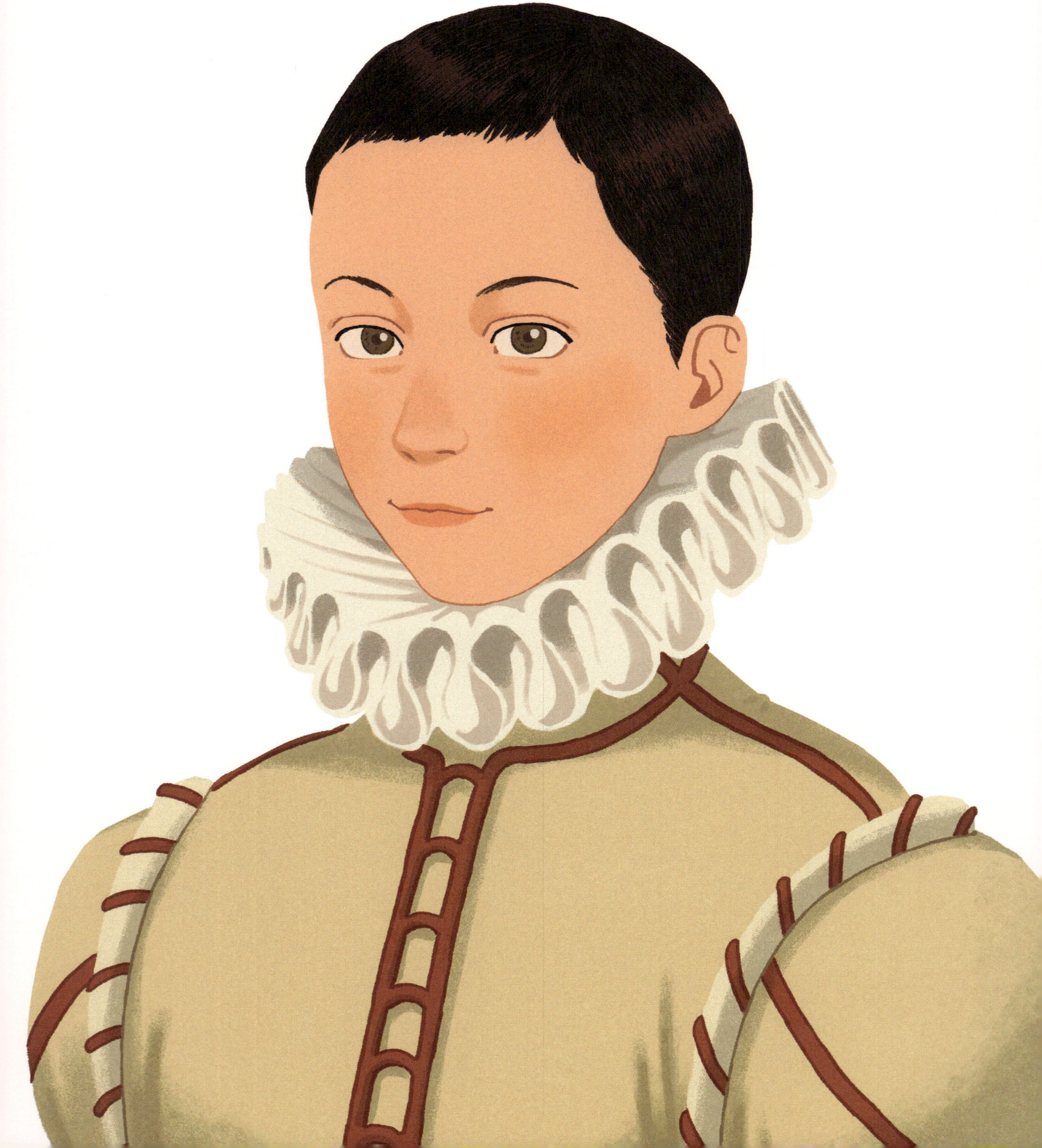

Saint Aloysius Gonzaga
(1568–1591)

The eldest son of an Italian noble family, the young Aloysius Gonzaga was promised a glorious future. Wealth, titles, and power were his for the taking. However, as a teenager, Aloysius started to wonder about the meaning of life. He began to think that true happiness was not to be found in this privileged existence.

Filled with Doubts

The surface of the water reflected the features of a thirteen-year-old boy, but Aloysius was not looking at his own image. Pensive, he studied the sumptuous Escorial Palace just completed for His Majesty King Philip II of Spain.

A pebble fell in the water, splashing his velvet jerkin.

"Aloysius, are you still daydreaming?" a voice asked behind him.

Aloysius turned around and smiled at his friend Felipe, a page like him.

"You have to go change!" Felipe pressed. "The ball starts in an hour."

Aloysius sighed. His hand plunged into the clear water and made pinwheels under the surface, blurring the reflection of the castle.

"What's the point?" he let out in a whisper.

"Excuse me?" Felipe asked, surprised.

"Dances, changing our doublets several times a day, the palace, the court life: What's the point of all this?" Aloysius inquired.

The other page was puzzled. "Well, to prepare for the future!" he said.

"My kingdom is not of this world," Aloysius muttered.

Stunned silence followed, so Aloysius added, "Jesus said this in the Gospels, not me!"

"Ah! I understand," said Felipe, though his surprised expression showed the opposite.

Aloysius turned away from the basin before adding, "I'm still trying to figure out where my kingdom is, what my duty is."

The Great Renouncement

"Father, please let me choose the path of priesthood. My heart is calling for it. Jesus is asking me."

Aloysius' voice resounded under the majestic ceilings of the Gonzaga residence in Castiglione, in the Duchy of Mantua, Italy. A long silence hovered before Duke Ferdinand I replied to his son, through a lump in his throat: "It's impossible, Aloysius. You're the eldest—"

"Of a large family," finished Aloysius. "I will willingly give up all my rights and titles. Rodolfo will bear them with great honor."

Ferdinand Gonzaga had a hard time letting go of all the plans he had for his eldest son. This path Aloysius wanted to follow, however, filled the heart of his mother, Marta, with great joy. She was the one who had raised him with such faith. Marta helped her husband to accept their son's vocation, and eventually, Ferdinand would even embrace it.

Aloysius, the Student

On November 2, 1585, during an official ceremony, Aloysius transferred all his privileges to his younger brother. Aloysius was seventeen. He was free. He immediately entered the novitiate of the Society of Jesus—the Jesuits, founded less than fifty years earlier by Ignatius of Loyola. The Society asked him to pursue his studies in Rome, and Aloysius fully devoted himself to this, finally seeing meaning in everything he was taught. He did not yet know where he would be sent to serve Jesus, but he didn't care. Although he had no motivation to serve the king of Spain, he would go to the end of the world for the service of God—and with great joy!

To Give Everything

"'To serve, to serve': that's all you talk about," the novice master complained. "But do you know, Aloysius, that to serve well you must first learn to obey?"

It was the year 1587. Since the day Aloysius Gonzaga entered the novitiate, he had already gotten into trouble a few times, and this wouldn't be the last. The education he had received in Castiglione trained him to command and gave him a fiery temperament. Aloysius did not always show humility and obedience, important virtues among the Jesuits.

"Excuse me, Father," he sighed. "I still have much progress to make."

"Put yourself in the school of Christ," replied the master of novices. "Meditate on the Gospels. See how our Lord became a servant and obeyed his Father."

Aloysius did his best to follow this advice. The example and the word of Jesus continued to make his faith grow, and to prepare him to give up everything—even his life—to answer the call of God.

Rome, June 1591. The streets are empty because of the plague.

No one goes out, for fear of getting sick.

However, Aloysius Gonzaga roams the city streets.

"Leave! There is nothing else you can do for him."

"What you do to the sick, you do to me."

Aloysius overcomes his revulsion and takes the patient to the hospital.

"Thank you."

"You have to heal now."

Everyone is treated with respect. Those who die leave in peace, with hope.

"Whoever loses his life for my sake will find it."

If I had to do it again, I would do the same thing, so these men don't die desperate and alone.

Aloysius catches the plague himself.

Aloysius went home to God on June 21, 1591.

ALOYSIUS, the Intrepid Student

Surname: Gonzaga
First name: Aloysius
Born: March 9, 1568, in Castiglione, Italy
Died: June 21, 1591, in Rome, Italy
Siblings: Nine brothers and sisters
Occupation: Page at the court of the king of Spain; later, novice in the Society of Jesus
Moments of weakness: At times found it hard to obey
Moments of strength: Overcame difficulties to serve Jesus

The Society of Jesus
Founded by Ignatius of Loyola after a long spiritual discernment, the Society of Jesus from the beginning set for itself the goal of being at the unconditional service of the pope and the Church everywhere in the world. The Jesuits complete a long formation before their ordination. At the time of Aloysius Gonzaga, many Jesuits became missionaries in Asia, America, and Africa.

☞ **ALOYSIUS GONZAGA** is the patron of Young people, students, and AIDS patients.

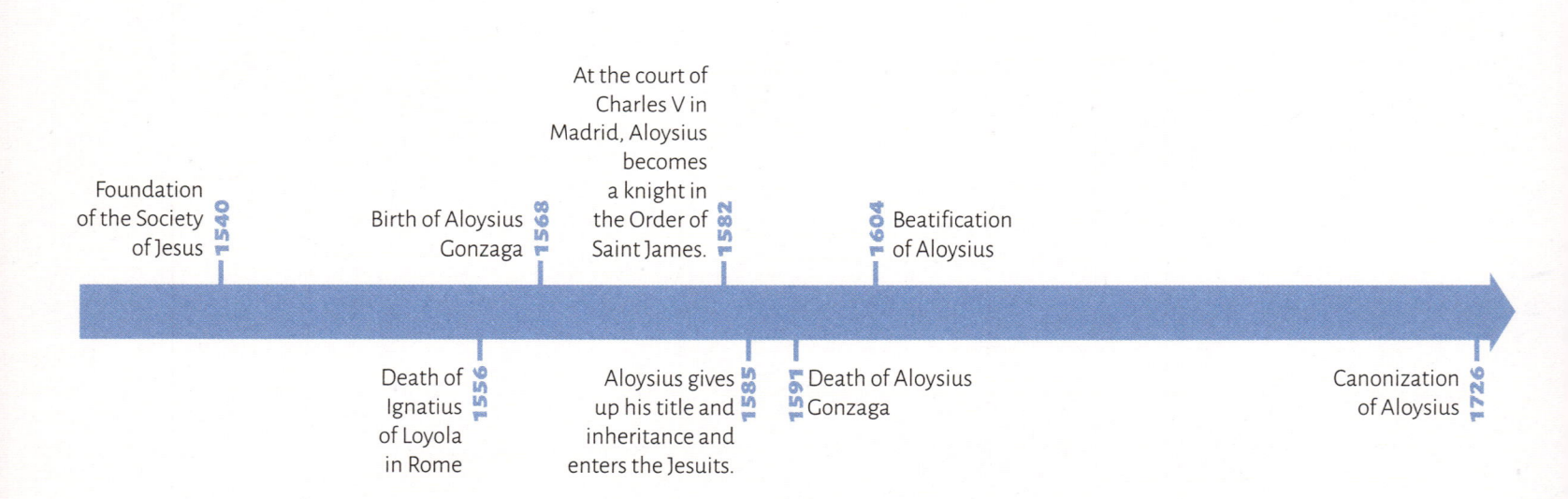

Timeline

- **1540** — Foundation of the Society of Jesus
- **1556** — Death of Ignatius of Loyola in Rome
- **1568** — Birth of Aloysius Gonzaga
- **1582** — At the court of Charles V in Madrid, Aloysius becomes a knight in the Order of Saint James.
- **1585** — Aloysius gives up his title and inheritance and enters the Jesuits.
- **1591** — Death of Aloysius Gonzaga
- **1604** — Beatification of Aloysius
- **1726** — Canonization of Aloysius

Prayer to Saint Aloysius Gonzaga

Saint Aloysius Gonzaga,
help us to let ourselves be formed by the Word of God.
You who wanted to serve God better and better,
help us to devote ourselves to God's way with enthusiasm,
so that we might become more like Jesus every day.

May your example help us to love our neighbor better,
to behave as true Christians
in our everyday life.

Protect the sick,
all the people who care for them with dedication,
all researchers who fight against serious diseases, and
all those who work to provide access to medical care
throughout the world today.
Amen.

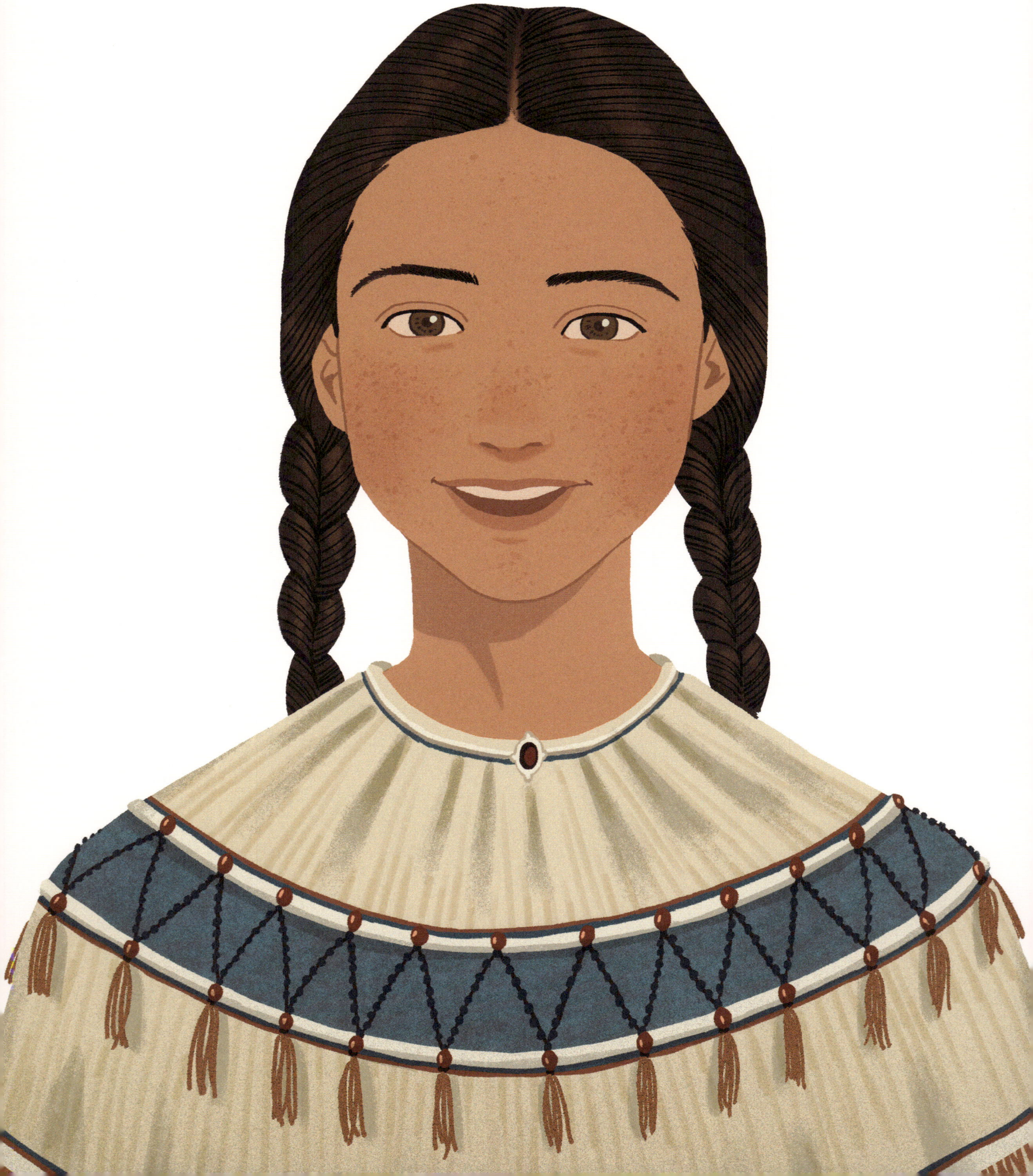

Saint Kateri Tekakwitha
(1656–1680)

"Bring salvation to the uttermost parts of the earth," Jesus told the first apostles (Acts 13:47). Kateri Tekakwitha's story is one of the great examples of the fulfillment of this command. Young Kateri was a member of the Mohawk people, in what is now New York State, and she discovered there in her own homeland the salvation, light, and peace that had originated in the Holy Land, far beyond the ocean.

The One Who Bumps into Things

It was the year 1661, and the valley was vibrant with an autumnal red. In the Mohawk village, an old woman sat on a rock, her four-year-old grandniece cuddled in her arms. Both turned their faces to the warm sunlight and were silent for a moment, enjoying the song of a nearby waterfall. Then the woman leaned over the child to touch her cheek gently. The little girl's skin, she thought, felt even more hardened and cracked than her own, worn by the years. She looked at the child's face: it was pockmarked with scars. The little girl was recovering from smallpox, a disease that had just claimed the lives of her young parents and brother.

The old woman sighed. She gestured at all the brilliant leaves around them.

"Can you see those fiery colors, Tekakwitha?" she asked.

Her people now called her Tekakwitha, "the one who bumps into things," because smallpox had damaged her eyesight.

"Yes, I see them," Tekakwitha replied.

The old woman noted with pleasure that the orphan was smiling again.

Three Strange Men

Years went by. Tekakwitha had been adopted by her uncle—a village chief—and two aunts. One morning, she saw three strange men approaching their longhouse, all dressed in black.

"Tekakwitha!" one of her aunts called in the distance. "Hurry up! I need your help with lunch!"

Tekakwitha was surprised at the anxious tone, and she wondered if her aunt really wanted to keep her away from these strangers. After a moment, she obeyed and ran to her aunt.

That night, she pretended to sleep as her two aunts whispered to one another.

"Christian missionaries," one said with disdain. "Her mother was raised by some of them. She believed in their God."

"Yes! She was an Algonquin," replied her other aunt with contempt. "We can't have any of this here. Our brother, her father, was a true Mohawk chief. One cannot be Mohawk and Christian."

Tell Me about Your God

"Did you hear that faint creak?" Father Pierron asked his two fellow Jesuits, as their campfire dwindled.

Father Frémin stood up, on guard. But the approaching shadow was not that of a coyote. As the figure came closer to the light of the flames, the men could see the face of a young native woman, etched with the scars of smallpox.

"Good evening," Father Pierron said, speaking the Iroquois language. "Do you need something?"

Tekakwitha answered with a question: "What does 'Christian' mean? My mother was a Christian. My aunts said so."

The priests exchanged a surprised look.

"Sit down," Father Frémin said. "We will answer your question, but it will take a little time!"

Tekakwitha the Luminous

More years passed. April 18, 1676, was a bright, sunny day, but it was nothing compared to the glow radiating in Tekakwitha's heart. The priest had just baptized her during Easter Mass, telling her with a smile, "You are now a child of God, and your name will be Kateri, Catherine."

What happiness! For years, ever since that first night when the Jesuit missionaries told her about Jesus' life, death, and resurrection, Kateri Tekakwitha had dreamed of devoting her life to the Lord. But her idea seemed impossible.

Continually mistreated for her faith and for refusing to wed, Tekakwitha fled her village in 1677, hiking hundreds of miles, across woods, mountains, and streams, to find refuge in the Catholic mission of Sault Saint Louis, in Quebec.

That day was the beginning of a new life. At twenty years old, free and baptized, she devoted herself entirely to Christ and began to share the faith by word, example, and friendship. She taught the Christian faith to children, cared for the poor and sick in the community, and was greatly beloved for her kindness of heart and her courage.

Centuries later, in 1980, Kateri was canonized a saint by Pope John Paul II. Her glow of faith still shines on in the Church to this day.

Saint Francis Xavier Mission, near the rapids of the Saint Lawrence River

Lost in thought, Father Claude?

Disappointed and sad... I feel useless.

I idealized this missionary life. People's hearts are closed here.

Come, let me introduce you to someone.

You'll see that you're wrong. Kateri's faith is stronger than ours.

The love of my life is Jesus.

Thank you for visiting me, Father.

Others help me to grow in faith.

Father Chauchetière comes regularly to Kateri's bedside.

You know, Kateri, it works both ways!

Father Chauchetière writes about the young Mohawk woman, and his testimony eventually leads to her canonization. Kateri reminds us that salvation has dawned for all people. Christ has died and risen for the whole world!

KATERI, *the Native American Disciple*

Birth name: Unknown
Name received at the death of her parents: Tekakwitha
Christian name: Kateri (Catherine)
Born: 1656, in Ossenon (now Auriesville), New York
Baptized: April 18, 1676
Died: April 17, 1680, in Kahnawake, Canada
Parents: Kenneronkwa and Kahenta
Siblings: A younger brother, who died of smallpox in 1661
Moments of weakness: Inflicted upon herself severe penances, against the advice of her priests
Moments of strength: Persevered through hardship, thanks to her faith

☞ **THE NORTH AMERICAN MARTYRS** In the decade before Tekakwitha's birth, several French Jesuit missionaries were killed by the Iroquois, including Saints René Goupil, Isaac Jogues, and Jean de Brebeuf. Father Brebeuf learned the language and culture of the Hurons, before the village he lived in was raided by the Iroquois. The North American Martyrs were canonized by Pope Pius XI in 1930.

Indigenous Peoples of the Saint Lawrence River, New York
Before the arrival of Europeans, several tribes lived in the area. The most well-known were the **Iroquois** (a group of five tribes, one of which was the Mohawks), the **Algonquins**, the **Hurons**, and the **Etchemins**.
Algonquins and Hurons were frequently at war against the Iroquois, who were said to be fearless warriors. Many of these wars were over the beaver fur trade. The colonization of North America by rival European countries also increased tensions.
Kateri Tekakwitha was the child of a marriage between an Iroquois and an Algonquin, which was exceptional at the time.

1534 Jacques Cartier discovers Canada.

1603 The Grand Alliance Treaty is signed between French explorer Samuel de Champlain and Native American leaders (Algonquins, Innus, and Etchemins). As a result, the French are able to establish Quebec and Montreal.

1650-1700 Wars between Iroquois and Algonquins

1656 Birth of Kateri Tekakwitha

1667 Peace is declared between the French and the Iroquois.

April 17, 1680 Death of Kateri Tekakwitha

Prayer to Saint Kateri Tekakwitha

Saint Kateri,
although your eyesight was weak,
you saw perfectly with the eyes of the heart
and walked with determination
on the path of faith.

Help us, like you, to be guided
by the Word of God,
by the hand of Jesus Christ.

Teach us to keep smiling even in hardship,
and to maintain an unshakeable confidence
in the wisdom of God watching over us.

Protect all Native Americans today,
and intercede for all the ethnic minorities of the world,
especially those who are threatened and abused.
Amen.

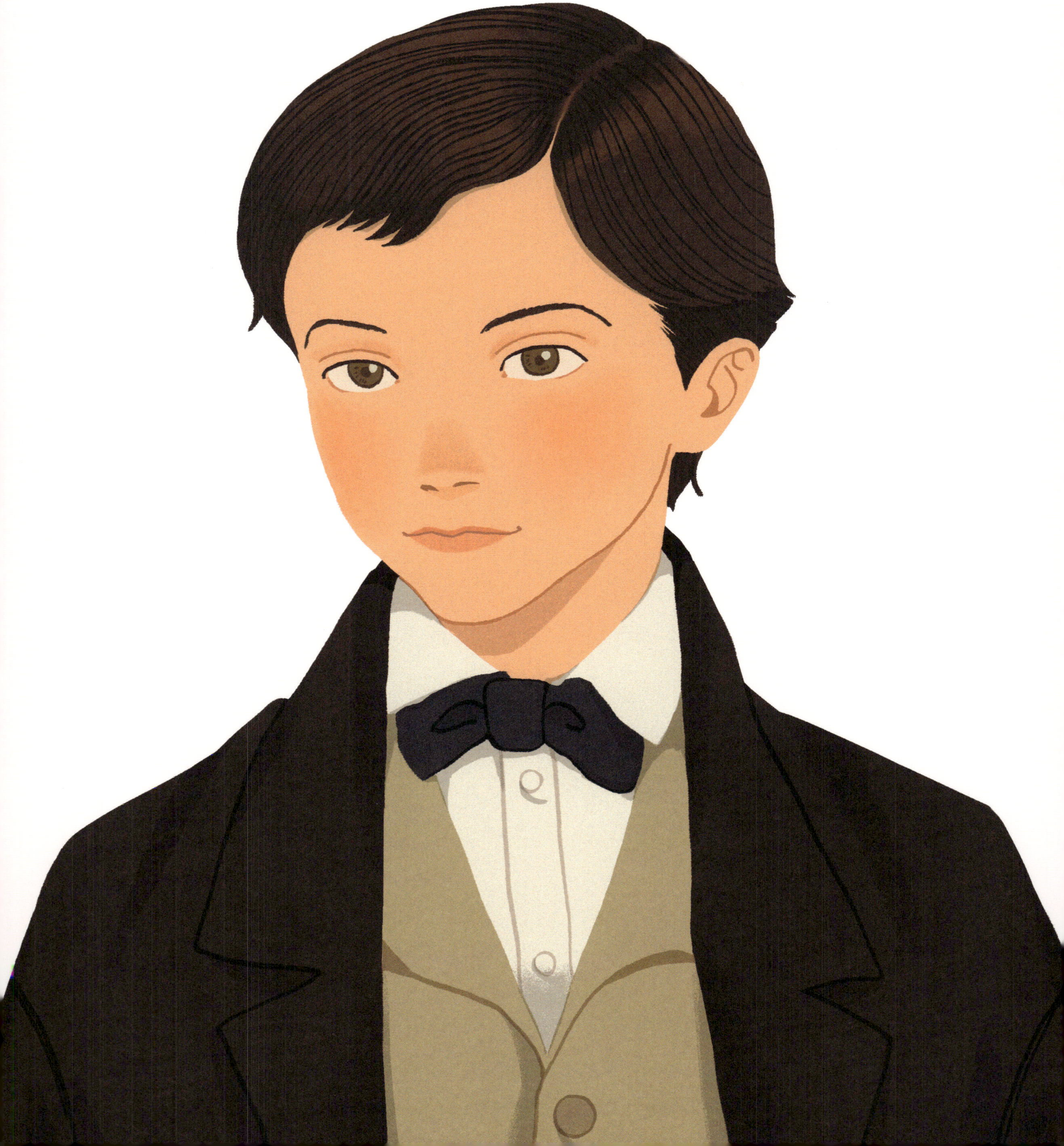

Saint Dominic Savio

(1842–1857)

In nineteenth-century Italy, Dominic was born into a poor, pious family. By age four, he already prayed many times daily, loved the Mass, and looked out for others. Back then, there were few opportunities for poor children to receive an education past elementary school; yet Dominic's parents wanted to give him this opportunity, and they reached out to the director of a boys' school in the big city of Turin. This would lead to a meeting between two great saints: Don Bosco and Dominic Savio.

A Sharp Boy

In October 1854, the priest John Bosco traveled to the small town of Murialdo, in northern Italy, with a group of boys from the city of Turin. They had come for fresh air and some quiet time in the country. Yet Father Bosco had another mission in mind: to meet a wise young boy he had heard about.

"Good afternoon, Father," the boy greeted him. "I am Dominic Savio and this is my father, Charles."

The priest smiled and greeted both father and son, then turned his attention to the boy. "Dominic, I have heard so many good things about you!"

The pastor in the nearby village of Mondonio had told him about Dominic—from his notable reverence for God to his peaceful demeanor and excellence in school. Father Bosco immediately found the boy friendly and easy to talk with. They spoke about Dominic's studies.

Then the priest asked: "What do you want to do in the future?"

"I really want to be a priest," Dominic confided.

"That's wonderful! Do you know that it requires a serious course of studies?"

"I do," Dominic replied.

"Good," said the priest, opening a little book from his pocket. "Let's find out how quickly you can learn. See this page? Memorize it while I chat with your father."

Less than ten minutes later, Dominic returned.

"I can recite it now if you want me to, Father."

"Ah, yes?" Father Bosco asked. "Go right ahead."

Dominic recited the entire page from memory, without a mistake.

"Well done!" exclaimed the priest. "Come to my school in Turin for your studies, if you want. May God help us both to do his holy will!"

First Time in Town

The crisp, dry air heralded autumn, but that wasn't what Dominic felt in his nostrils. In the working-class neighborhood of Valdocco in Turin, black coal smoke poured from the chimneys, a scent unfamiliar to the new young resident.

"Hi, Dominic!" an upperclassman greeted him. "Don Bosco told us about you. You made a big impression on him." ("Don" is an Italian title of respect.)

"You will have to start playing ball with us and beef up a little!" another student said.

"Leave him alone," one of the boys remarked. "He's skinny, but he must be strong. Don Bosco says he used to walk six hours a day, to school and back, all by himself."

"That's true, but I wasn't alone," Dominic replied. "My guardian angel is always with me."

His words were met with a stunned silence.

"What?" he added, a little snicker at the corner of his lips. "Isn't that true?"

An Instrument of Peace

Angry cries caught Dominic's attention, and he opened the library window.

In the yard, two boys were arguing and shoving each other. Everyone knew Gianni and Giuiseppe couldn't get along.

After a few seconds, they started rolling on the ground, punching each other. Dominic rushed out the door, just as Giuseppe walked away after a heavy thump to Gianni's stomach. But Gianni got up and picked up a rock. "Turn around if you're a man!" he yelled.

Giuseppe turned around and also picked up a stone.

But an obstacle stood in the way. Dominic had jumped between them.

"Move!" Gianni yelled.

"No way," Dominic replied. "You'll have to throw the first stone at me."

Both boys, ashamed before their classmate's courageous stand, dropped their stones at the same time and walked away in opposite directions.

Despite Dominic's slender frame, there was something about him that gave him more power than anyone else. It wasn't his good grades or his seriousness in class. Rather, the whole school was certain this boy lived in the company of Jesus. And he received Jesus as often as possible in the Eucharist, growing closer to him every day.

June 24, 1855. The city of Turin celebrates the Feast of Saint John the Baptist, its patron saint!

The school of Don Bosco also celebrates this special day.

Don Bosco promises to offer to his students a gift of their choice.

— Chocolate!

Chocolate, cheese, cold cuts, and so on...

— Sliced salami—is that you, Francesco?

— "Help me to become a saint."

— Really?

This request is signed "Dominic."

— The secret of holiness is, first of all, joy. Then come studies, prayer, and service to others.

— Thanks, Father.

— Savio, take care of yourself.
— I feel good today.

All through eighth grade, despite his fragile health, Dominic follows Don Bosco's advice.

— Oh! What I see is so beautiful!

March 9, 1857. Dominic dies of tuberculosis. His last words show his family that he achieved his goal: he became a saint.

33

DOMINIC, Holiness —and Quick!

Surname: Savio
First name: Dominic (Domenico, in Italian)
Born: April 2, 1842, in Turin, Italy
Died: March 9, 1857, in Mondonio, Italy
Parents: Carlo Savio and Brigida Gaiato
Siblings: Nine
Life goal: To be a priest and a saint
Moment of weakness: Sadness when his illness took him away from his friends
Moment of strength: Courage in living his faith at school

A Pair of Saints

Saint John Bosco (1815–1888) was an Italian priest who devoted his entire life to the education of youth, especially the poor children of Turin—a working-class city with harsh social inequalities at the time of the Industrial Revolution.

Popularly known as Don Bosco, he met Dominic Savio through a priest, during a stay in his hometown. The two saints were true "neighbors," born in villages located about two miles away from each other. Don Bosco took Dominic under his wing and looked after his education with great care. Known throughout the world, the two saints are often associated.

Did You Know?

Dominic Savio is the patron saint of young criminals (because he helped several friends in trouble to rediscover the faith). He is also the patron saint of choirboys.

☞ **GOING TO SCHOOL: A CHOICE** In 1859, school became mandatory in the Piedmont region of Italy, where Dominic Savio lived. The daily six miles that Dominic walked to get to and from school was voluntary. His parents knew his thirst and gift for learning, so they allowed him to make this trek.

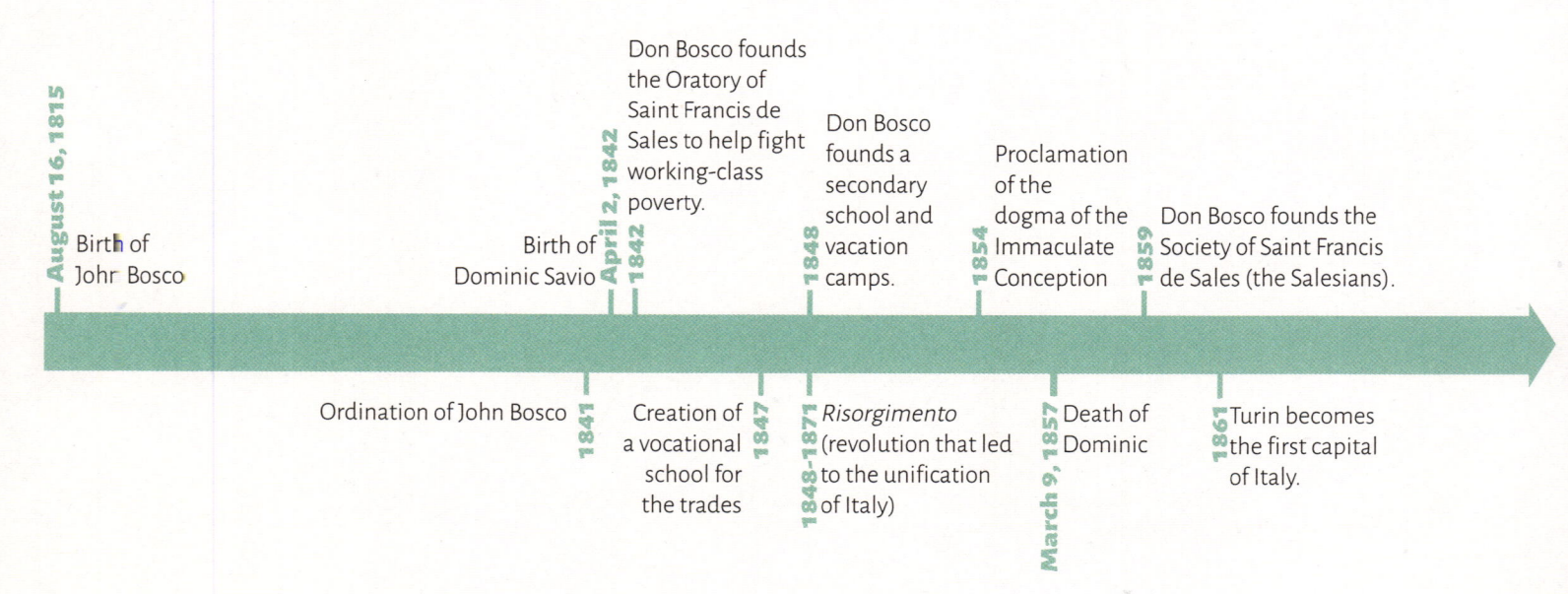

Timeline (above):
- August 16, 1815 — Birth of John Bosco
- April 2, 1842 — Birth of Dominic Savio
- 1842 — Don Bosco founds the Oratory of Saint Francis de Sales to help fight working-class poverty.
- 1848 — Don Bosco founds a secondary school and vacation camps.
- 1854 — Proclamation of the dogma of the Immaculate Conception
- 1859 — Don Bosco founds the Society of Saint Francis de Sales (the Salesians).

Timeline (below):
- 1841 — Ordination of John Bosco
- 1847 — Creation of a vocational school for the trades
- 1848–1871 — *Risorgimento* (revolution that led to the unification of Italy)
- March 9, 1857 — Death of Dominic
- 1861 — Turin becomes the first capital of Italy.

34

Prayer to Saint Dominic Savio

Saint Dominic,
you who were known for always having a smile,
inspire us so that we smile too.

Help us reflect to those around us
the joy of believing and the joy of living.

Watch over students around the world,
especially over victims of bullying
at school, online, or on social media.

You who always defended those who were mocked,
help us to stand up for others and refuse to tolerate
injustice, meanness, and insults at school.
Help us to act always as true Christians.
Amen.

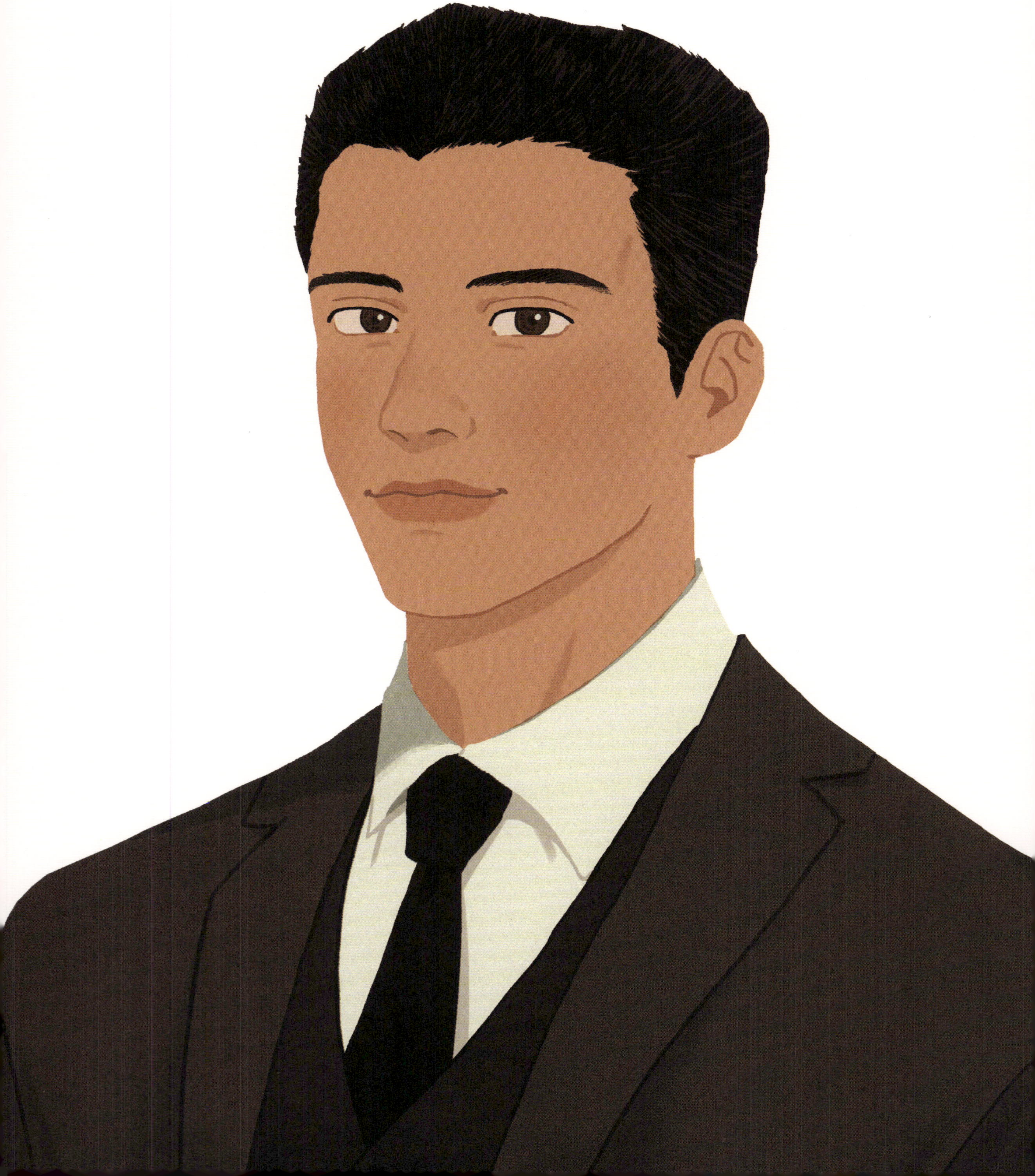

Blessed Pier Giorgio Frassati
(1901–1925)

Pier Giorgio was a fun, athletic, and friendly boy, and yet his parents were worried. Why refuse to choose a prosperous career? Why avoid all family receptions and social events? The life of Pier Giorgio was full of mysteries, until it all became clear in the summer of 1925.

A Little Boy with a Big Heart

"Alfredo, I think I heard someone knocking," Mrs. Frassati said, her paintbrush moving across the canvas, creating a mountain landscape.

As her husband went to open the door, their son, Pier Giorgio, followed behind him, across the elegant rooms of the Frassati residence. The man at the door had a worn-out face. He seemed old, poor, and dirty. The child noticed his father draw back slightly, repulsed.

"Mercy!" the beggar said in a hoarse voice.

His breath smelled of wine, and Alfredo Frassati closed the door, grimacing.

Pier Giorgio burst into tears and ran to his mother, Adélaïde.

"Mama, it's our duty to help the poor. God asks us to!"

Up on the Mountain

Summer 1912. The snowcapped peak of Mount Castor sparkled under the blue sky. At 2,600 miles up, Pier Giorgio felt great happiness contemplating the mountains and valleys that endlessly unfolded around him.

"It's time to go back down," his mother told him, her hand on his shoulder.

"What, already?"

"There are many other summits for you to see, Pier Giorgio. Now that you're eleven, you're old enough to start hiking and even climbing."

"Yes. It feels close to heaven here. Close to God!"

Mrs. Frassati smiled. Her son's faith touched her, even if she didn't share it very deeply. She went to Mass more out of duty than desire, and her husband did not even come with her. But for Pier Giorgio, prayer was a spontaneous joy, especially since his First Communion last year.

A Little Embarrassing, Pier Giorgio!

Summer 1921. The sounds of the party started to fade; the last guests were going home. The host saw the son of her friends Alfredo and Adélaïde approaching.

"Thank you, *Signora*." Pier Giorgio said. "What a wonderful evening!"

"You came late," she remarked. "Did you still have fun?"

"My apologies," the young man answered. "I had a lot of work."

"Are your parents well in Berlin?" the hostess asked. "Does your father enjoy his work as ambassador?"

"Yes, my father is happy to serve our country! May I ask you, what you plan to do with those magnificent flowers?" Pier Giorgio inquired, pointing to the dozens of bouquets adorning the large living room.

"I don't know! We are drowning in flowers," she said with a quick look around.

"Would you give me some?"

The question was a bit indelicate, but she nodded kindly.

She knew Pier Giorgio well enough to be prepared for his lack of manners in society. It was something that troubled his parents. What no one knew was that if he was often late, it was because of his daily visits to the poor of Turin—feeding them, buying them medicine, and bringing them clothes. No one suspected, either, that he used secondhand bouquets to decorate their graves when they died.

Life Is Beautiful

1923. Pier Giorgio was in the mountains again. This hike did him a lot of good, as usual. Looking at the landscape from up there, it felt like a retreat, giving him an aerial view of his life.

He had dedicated his engineering studies to God with the idea of one day working in a factory with the working class. He kept visiting the poor; his life of faith was nourished by the Mass and prayer. Pier Giorgio felt happy, despite many reasons for sadness. The rise of Fascism in Italy worried him as much as it worried his father. Alfredo Frassati had resigned from his post as ambassador so as not to represent a government he now hated. What would become of Italy under the leadership of the dictator Benito Mussolini?

It was so beautiful here in the mountains. Sometimes it was good to leave all worrying thoughts down in the plain. Pier Giorgio focused on all the reasons to be optimistic. He was young, strong, happy, and surrounded by good friends and a crowd of poor people who were like his second family. Yes, life was good for a Christian like him.

June 1925

"Great! Lock me!"

"You all right, Pier Giorgio?"

"At the top! Good job!"

"Thanks, Pier Giorgio. This is amazing."

"Do you want to come to Mario's party tomorrow?"

"I can't... I've got something to do."

Pier Giorgio had promised to visit a poor family.

"I'm bringing the medications that the doctor prescribed."

"How can we thank you?"

June 29, 1925. Pier Giorgio feels exhausted. He doesn't complain, thinking it's the flu.

"Please go bring these medications for me..."

Suffering from polio contracted through his contact with the poor, he died on July 4, 1925, still taking care of his friends until the end.

A big crowd showed up at his funeral.

"You didn't know that Pier Giorgio was a friend to all the poor people of Turin? Your son is a saint!"

Pope John Paul II, a hiker and mountaineer as well, beatified Pier Giorgio in 1990. He declared Pier Giorgio the patron saint of World Youth Day.

PIER GIORGIO, *from Mountain to Heaven*

Surname: Frassati
First name: Pier Giorgio
Born: April 6, 1901, in Turin, Italy
Died: July 4, 1925, in Turin, Italy
Father: Alfredo Frassati (newspaper publisher, senator, ambassador)
Mother: Adélaïde Ametis (painter)
Siblings: Two sisters (Elda, who died in infancy, and Luciana, who died in 2007)
Education: Polytechnic University of Turin (mining engineering)
Moments of weakness: Trouble with manners and punctuality
Moments of strength: Heroic charity for the poor
Patron of: World Youth Day

☞ **WHAT IS A THIRD ORDER?** It is an association of lay Christians who feel spiritually close to a religious order and live by its rules, although adapted to their secular lives. The Dominican Third Order, of which Pier Giorgio was a member, is close to the Order of Preachers founded by Saint Dominic in the thirteenth century. There is also a Franciscan Third Order and a Carmelite Third Order, among others.

Saint Vincent de Paul Conferences

Founded in Paris in 1833 by a few lay students, including Blessed Frédéric Ozanam, Saint Vincent de Paul Conferences are groups of Christians who organize themselves to respond to poverty in their neighborhoods. They provide aid to the poor; visit the sick, elderly, or lonely; support the education of poor children; and do other charitable works. Pier Giorgio was a member of a Conference in Turin. Although discreet, Saint Vincent de Paul Conferences make an impressive impact. About eight hundred thousand volunteers spanning five continents help thirty million people on a daily basis.

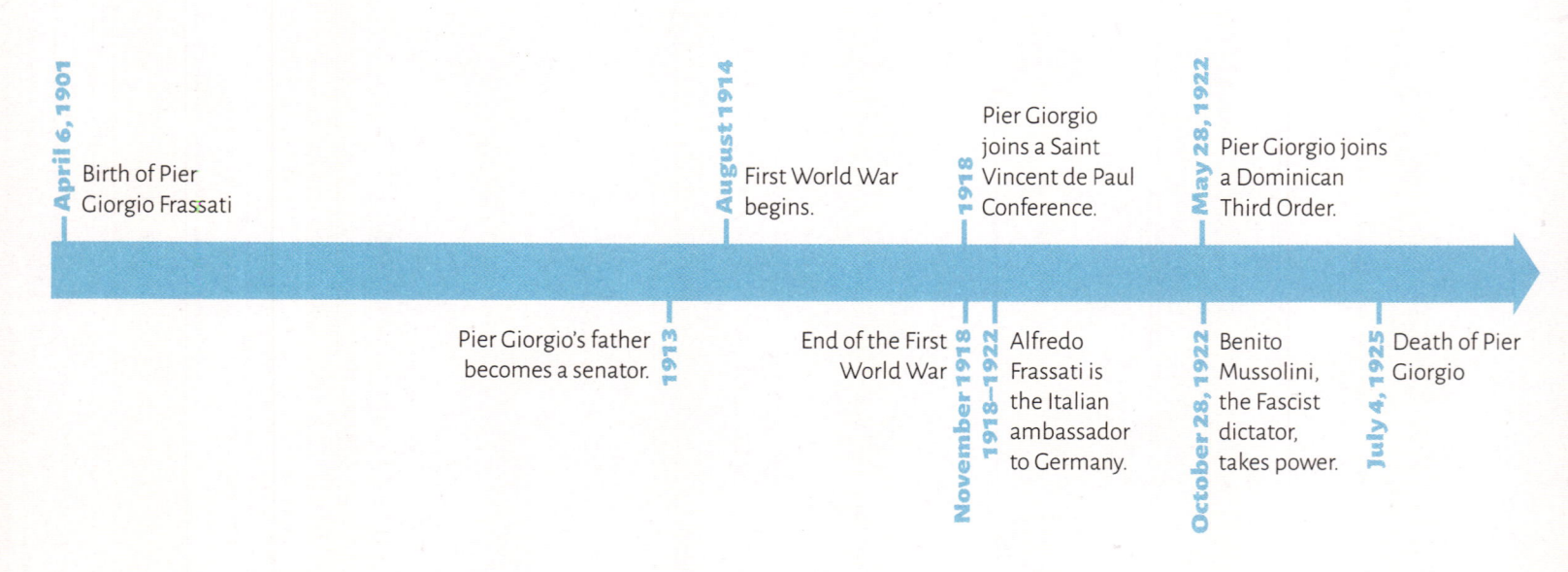

Timeline:

- **April 6, 1901:** Birth of Pier Giorgio Frassati
- **1913:** Pier Giorgio's father becomes a senator.
- **August 1914:** First World War begins.
- **November 1918:** End of the First World War
- **1918:** Pier Giorgio joins a Saint Vincent de Paul Conference.
- **1918–1922:** Alfredo Frassati is the Italian ambassador to Germany.
- **May 28, 1922:** Pier Giorgio joins a Dominican Third Order.
- **October 28, 1922:** Benito Mussolini, the Fascist dictator, takes power.
- **July 4, 1925:** Death of Pier Giorgio

Prayer to Blessed Pier Giorgio Frassati

Blessed Pier Giorgio,
your phrase "to the heights"
describes the way you lived.
Teach us to embrace these words as our motto,
doing the will of God,
which will lead us to heaven.

Help us not to slip
down the slopes of mediocrity,
selfishness, or vanity.
Rather, inspire us to elevate our souls
by asking God to increase in us
goodness and generosity.

Help us to walk joyfully in this life
and to share our joy far and wide,
especially by caring for those
who are poor, fragile, lonely, or sick.

Now that you have arrived on the Holy Mountain,
pray to the Lord for all the volunteers
who are helping their neighbors right now.
Amen.

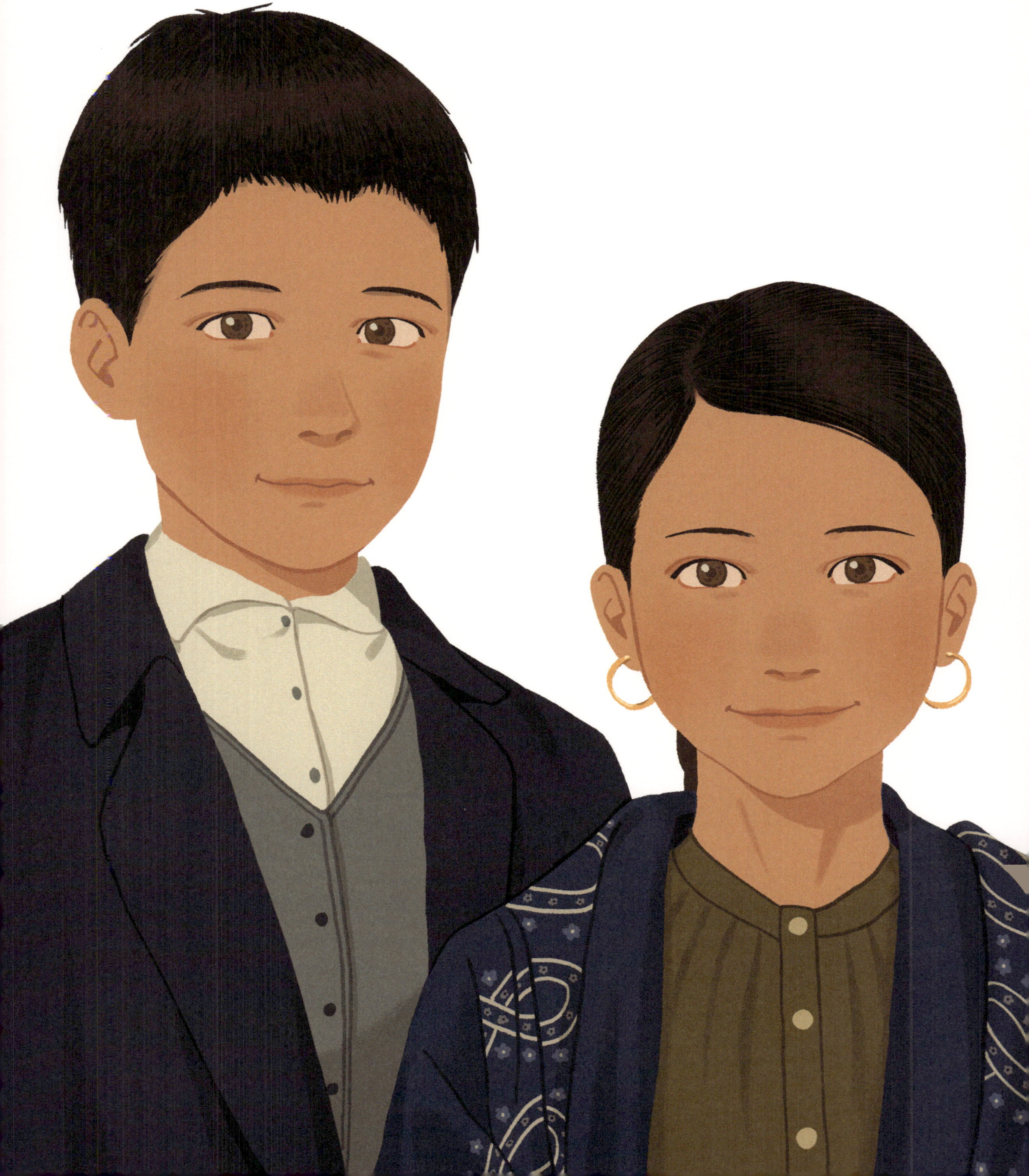

Saints Francisco and Jacinta Marto

(1908–1919, 1910–1920)

Francisco and his sister Jacinta, only eight and six years old, were tending their parents' sheep with their cousin Lucia in the countryside near Fatima, Portugal. The year was 1916, and in those days, schooling was not yet mandatory. It was springtime, and as the children were enjoying a warm, sunny day, they saw an apparition.

Like a Statue of Snow

Francisco, Jacinta, and Lucia had just finished their lunch and their shortened version of the Rosary. They would say only the first two words of each Our Father and Hail Mary in order to spend more time having fun. Francisco would play his flute, and the girls would sing and dance.

A sudden gust of wind caught their attention, and a radiant being stood before them. He looked like a young man, and he was whiter than snow.

"Don't be afraid," he said. "I am the Angel of Peace."

The Angel's Prayer

The celestial visitor appeared to them two more times times over the following months. In this year with the First World War in full swing, he taught them to say this prayer: "My God, I believe, I adore, I hope, and I love you! I ask pardon of you for those who do not believe, do not adore, do not hope, and do not love you."

The children no longer thought of shortening their Rosary. Praying had become more than a duty: it was a joy. The light radiating from the angel illuminated their lives. But they did not know that another celestial visitor would soon come to Fatima.

The Lady

On May 13, 1917, Jacinta was in the meadows of Cova da Iria, near Fatima. Francisco and Lucia were there with her tending sheep. At noon, she was looking at a holm oak tree, when her dark eyes suddenly widened in astonishment. A small, light cloud had landed on the little tree, and on it stood the most beautiful person Jacinta had ever seen: a lady dressed in white, who gazed at her like a mother.

A swift glance to both sides assured her that Francisco and Lucia saw the woman too. Was this the lady they were praying to when saying their Rosary?

Jacinta heard the woman speak with Lucia and ask her to pray for peace in the world and for the conversion of sinners. It seemed like a dream, only far more beautiful. Jacinta listened carefully to the dialogue. Francisco could not hear the words, but his eyes witnessed this extraordinarily lovely vision.

On Time to the Meetings

July 13, 1917. The entire region was buzzing with rumors: since May, on the thirteenth day of each month, three young shepherds from Fatima had been visited by a Lady who might be the Blessed Virgin. Would she show up for this third meeting?

A big crowd had gathered in the meadow, but some were skeptical and made fun of the children. Even priests and bishops remained cautious and refused to give their approval to these alleged apparitions.

Ignoring the din around them, Jacinta, Lucia, and Francisco were kneeling, immersed in praying the Rosary. Then, all of a sudden, their faces lit up.

"There she is!" they exclaimed.

The graceful Lady talked to the children for a long time.

"Keep praying," she told them. "Say the Rosary every day in honor of Our Lady of the Rosary, and pray for peace in the world."

Toward the end of the meeting, Lucia respectfully asked her how to convince people that the apparitions were real.

The Lady answered with a promise: on October 13, there would be a miracle.

October 13, 1917.
It has been raining all morning.

"There she is!"
"The sun is coming out!"

"It is a miracle!"
"The sun is dancing!"

The miracle causes a sensation. Jacinta, Francisco, and Lucia do not see it; they are too busy contemplating the Virgin.

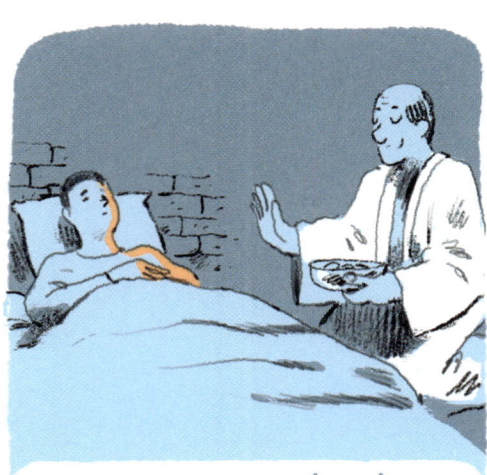

The children continue to pray for the end of the war. That finally happens in 1918.

"Lord, may peace return!"

Tragically, a terrible epidemic of Spanish flu breaks out. The Martos get sick.

Francisco is called to God first, followed by Jacinta about ten months later.

Fatima becomes a center of pilgrimage and is famous around the world. It touches and transforms the hearts of many.

On May 13, 2017, exactly one hundred years after the first apparition of Our Lady of the Rosary, Francisco and Jacinta are canonized by Pope Francis.

45

FRANCISCO AND JACINTA, *the Shepherds of Fatima*

Surname: Marto
First names: Francisco and Jacinta
Born: June 11, 1908 (Francisco), and March 11, 1910 (Jacinta), in Fátima, Portugal
Died: April 4, 1919, in Fátima, Portugal (Francisco), and February 20, 1920, in Lisbon, Portugal (Jacinta)
Parents: Manuel Marto and Olympia Marto
Occupation: Shepherds
Francisco's talent: Music (pan flute)
Jacinta's talents: Dance, poetry
Patrons of: Prisoners

☞ **FRANCISCO AND JACINTA AS SEEN BY THEIR COUSIN LUCIA** Lucia became a Carmelite nun and lived to the age of ninety-seven years old; she died in 2005. Asked about the personality of her cousins, here is what she said: "Francisco was a good, thoughtful child with a contemplative soul; Jacinta was lively, rather sensitive, but very sweet and loving."

The ancient pastures of Fatima have become a sanctuary: **the Basilica of Our Lady of the Rosary at Fatima**. Its first stone was laid in 1928. The pilgrimage center has grown over the decades, with the addition of an esplanade, a second basilica, and welcome centers. Every year the sanctuary of Fatima accommodates around six million pilgrims.

Did You Know?

The Miracle of the Sun

On October 13, 1917, about seventy thousand people gathered at Fatima to wait for the miracle that the Blessed Virgin Mary had promised. It was raining hard all day, and then suddenly the sky cleared and the sun came out, drying up all the water on the ground. The sun became incredibly clear and bright and colorful, and it began to move in the sky as if dancing. Thousands of people claimed to have seen the phenomenon. And yet the country's observatories did not detect any unusual activity of the sun at that time. Opinions therefore remain divided on this miracle which—like any miracle—requires faith.

Timeline:

- **June 11, 1908** — Birth of Francisco Marto
- **March 11, 1910** — Birth of Jacinta Marto
- **October 5, 1910** — Revolution in Portugal. King Manuel II flees. A new republic is proclaimed, beginning a period of instability in the country, along with great poverty.
- **August 1914** — Beginning of the First World War
- **March 1916** — First apparition of the Angel of Peace
- **May 13, 1917** — First apparition of the Virgin Mary at Fatima
- **October 13, 1917** — Sixth and last apparition of the Virgin Mary at Fatima
- **1918** — End of the First World War. Spanish flu epidemic begins.
- **1919** — Death of Francisco
- **1920** — Death of Jacinta

Prayer to Saint Jacinta and Saint Francisco

Saints Jacinta and Francisco,
teach us to pray with your fervor.
Help us to live with our hearts turned toward God,
in the light of his love.

You who prayed so much on earth for the conversion of sinners,
help us to say no to sin,
to recognize that we are very small before the Lord,
and to draw close to him.

Pray for our world,
still ravaged by war,
and ask God to make his peace reign in the hearts of all people.

Our Lady of Fatima,
with Jacinta and Francisco
and their cousin Lucia,
pray for us.
Amen.

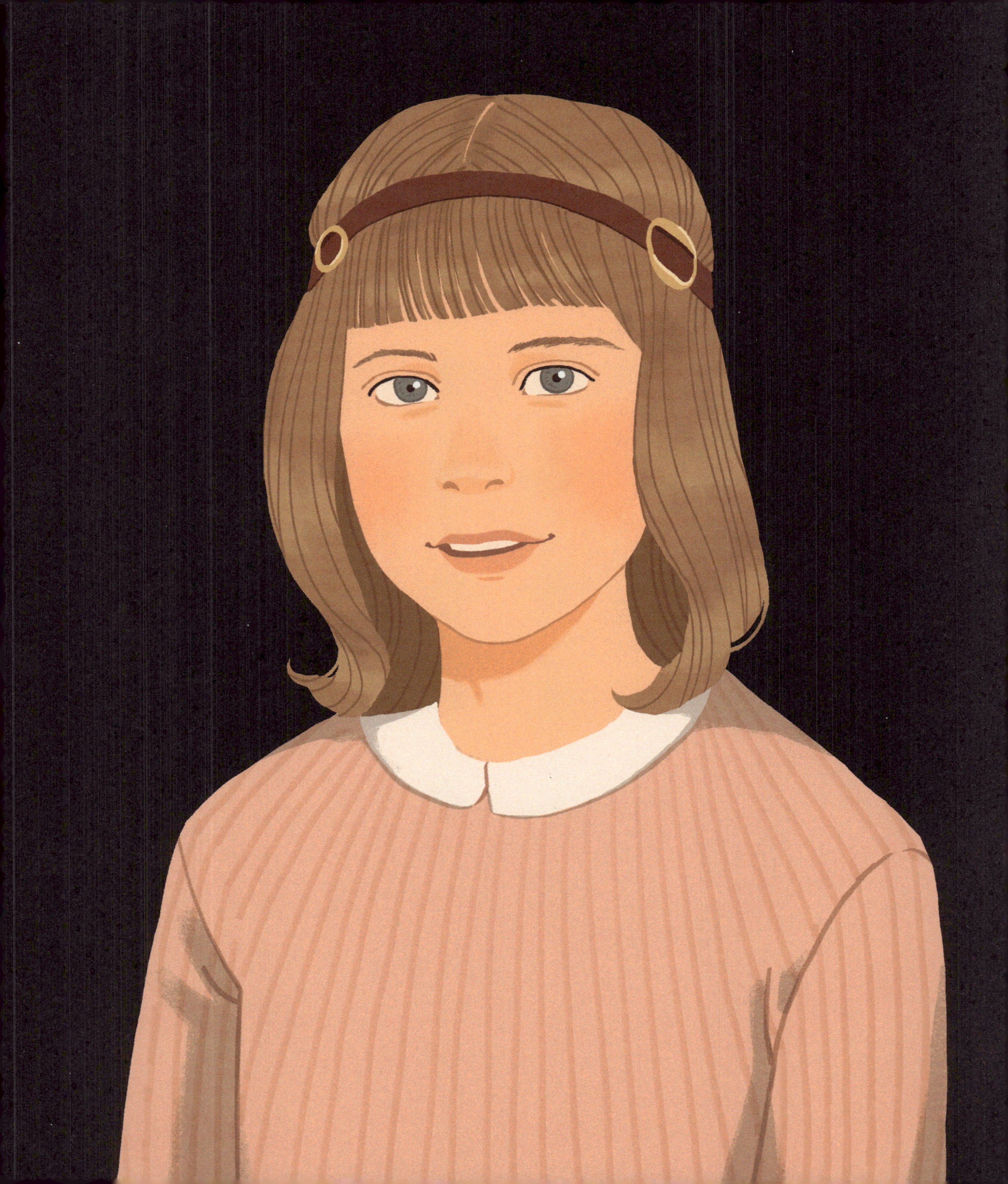

Venerable Anne de Guigné
(1911–1922)

This is the story of a little girl who once seemed quite far from holiness. Often obnoxious to her brother and sisters, disobedient to her parents, angry, and envious, she was feared by everyone in the upper-class French castle where the de Guigné family lived. Yet, this is also the story of the grace of God, for whom nothing is impossible.

One More Tantrum

Christmas 1914. In spite of the warm, crackling fire, it felt chilly in the big living room, and the mood was not cheerful; someone was missing. Jacques de Guigné—the father of Anne, Jacques, Magdeleine, and a baby on the way—had been away at war since August.

Grandpa had done everything he could to make Christmas merry. The gifts were nicely propped in front of the fireplace for everyone to enjoy.

Then three-and-a-half-year-old Anne ran to her present—a pretty wooden chair for her playroom.

"Oh! What a wonderful little chair!" her mother exclaimed, with a little nod to the child's grandfather to thank him. But Anne was frowning. She had her eyes on her cousin, who had just unwrapped a tiny table.

"It's not fair!" she yelled, stomping her feet. "I want that table!"

Everyone froze. These tantrums had become quite frequent lately—and so unpredictable! Without a word, the grandfather left the room, trying not to show his annoyance.

The Terrible News

On July 30, 1915, Anne's mother woke her up with tears in her eyes. At once, Anne understood that something terrible had happened.

Her mother took her in her arms and held her tight. "Your papa," she said with a broken voice, "he won't be coming back."

Jacques de Guigné had fallen in battle.

The shock of her father's death was enormous for the four-year-old girl.

Looking for consolation, Anne and her mother went to Mass together. God alone can help in times like this.

"What can I do to console you, Mama?" she asked.

Antoinette de Guigné looked at her daughter and said in a serious but tender tone: "If you want to console me, try to be good."

These words penetrated deep down in the soul of the angry and haughty little girl. Anne decided to change. She knew she wouldn't be able to do it alone, but she knew whom to ask for help.

Transformed

That winter of 1916, Antoinette, whose health had been fragile since the death of her husband, moved with her children to Cannes, in the south of France. Anne was now five years old. In a year's time, she had completely transformed. No one could believe she would have ever thrown tantrums.

"Anne? Angry? Impossible!"

It was her friendship with Jesus that helped Anne to change. She had decided to be the best friend she could to Jesus and never to leave him again. She wished to become a Carmelite someday.

But for the moment, she was eager to make her First Communion, although she was still only a small girl. The nuns in charge of her catechism presented the idea to Father Perroy, a Jesuit priest.

"She is too young," said the priest, skeptical.

"Ask her questions and you'll see," the sisters answered.

Father Perroy quizzed Anne, and by the end of the meeting, he agreed: "I wish everyone had a religious knowledge as good as this little girl!"

Anne received the Eucharist on March 26, 1917.

This strengthened even more the little girl's friendship with Jesus.

Cannes, January 1922

Every year, Anne's family spends the winter in southern France.

Tragically, at the end of December, Anne becomes sick with meningitis.

"Don't cry, Mama! I don't like seeing you sad."

"I tried to be better, just for you."

"You did so great! Anne, you're my little ray of sunshine."

After years of praying to her guardian angel, Anne can now hear him calling her.

"Sister, can I go with the angels?"

"Yes, my dear, you can."

Anne's strong will gave her life the speed and power of a lightning bolt. May she inspire us!

ANNE DE GUIGNÉ, the Girl Who Tamed Her Anger

Surname: de Guigné
First name: Anne
Born: April 25, 1911, in Annecy, France
Died: January 14, 1922, in Cannes, France
Parents: Jacques and Antoinette de Guigné
Siblings: Jacques, Magdeleine, and Marie-Antoinette
Moments of weakness: Jealousy and angry outbursts in her early childhood
Moments of strength: Conversion through prayer, comforting her mother

Did You Know?

Because of Anne de Guigné's admirable spiritual path, Pope John Paul II proclaimed her venerable in 1990.

☞ **CHILDREN'S COMMUNION** Before 1910, children had to wait until twelve years of age to receive their First Communion. But on August 8, 1910, Pope Pius X signed the decree *Quam Singulari*, authorizing children to make their First Communion at the age of seven. This decision was inspired by the story of four-year-old Ellen Organ, from Ireland, who died from tuberculosis in 1908. Shortly before Ellen's death, her bishop authorized her to receive the Eucharist she had been asking for so insistently.

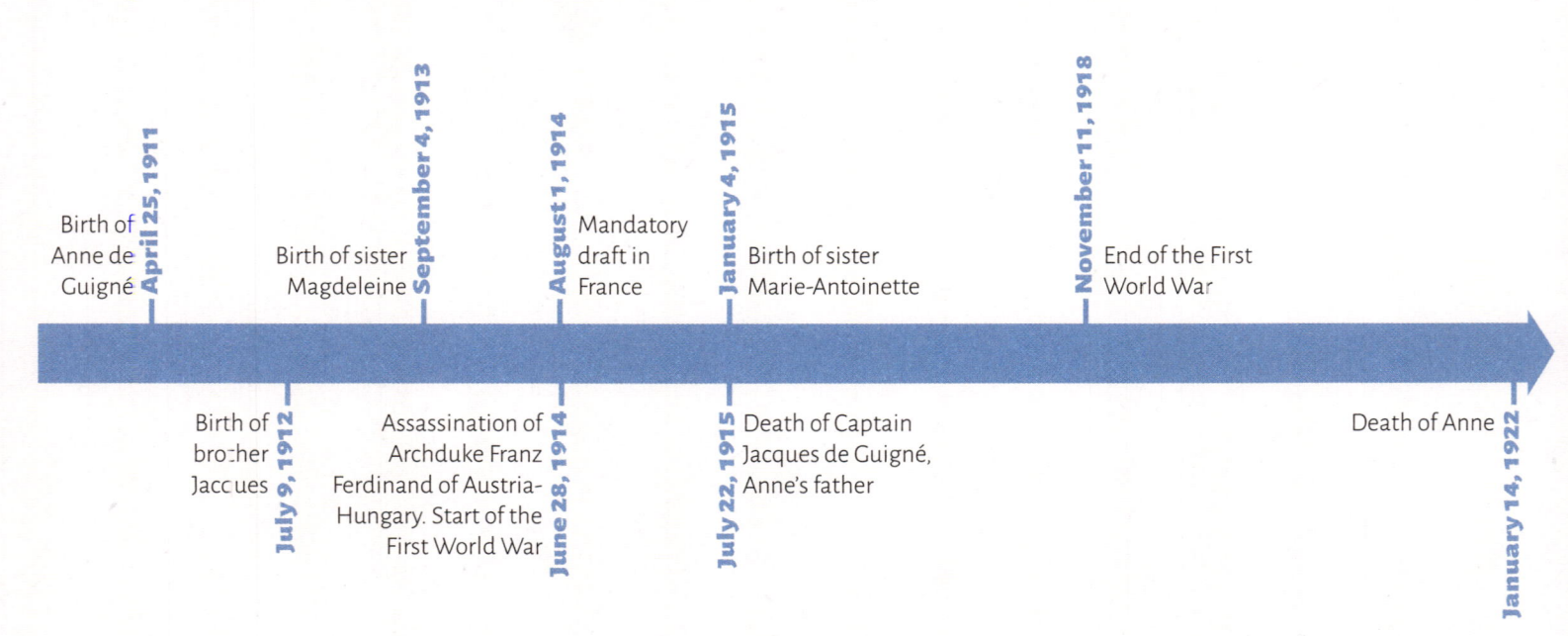

Timeline

- **April 25, 1911** — Birth of Anne de Guigné
- **July 9, 1912** — Birth of brother Jacques
- **September 4, 1913** — Birth of sister Magdeleine
- **June 28, 1914** — Assassination of Archduke Franz Ferdinand of Austria-Hungary. Start of the First World War
- **August 1, 1914** — Mandatory draft in France
- **January 4, 1915** — Birth of sister Marie-Antoinette
- **July 22, 1915** — Death of Captain Jacques de Guigné, Anne's father
- **November 11, 1918** — End of the First World War
- **January 14, 1922** — Death of Anne

Prayer to Anne de Guigné

Venerable Anne,
you knew how to fight against your faults
by asking Jesus for help every day
and trying your best.
You progressed quickly
on the way to holiness.
You were just a child,
not accomplishing anything spectacular
in the eyes of the world.
And yet, you attempted the bravest feat:
you invited God to change your heart,
and you welcomed his action in you.
Help us to do the same,
out of love for our parents,
our family, and our friends,
all in the love of Jesus Christ.
Amen.

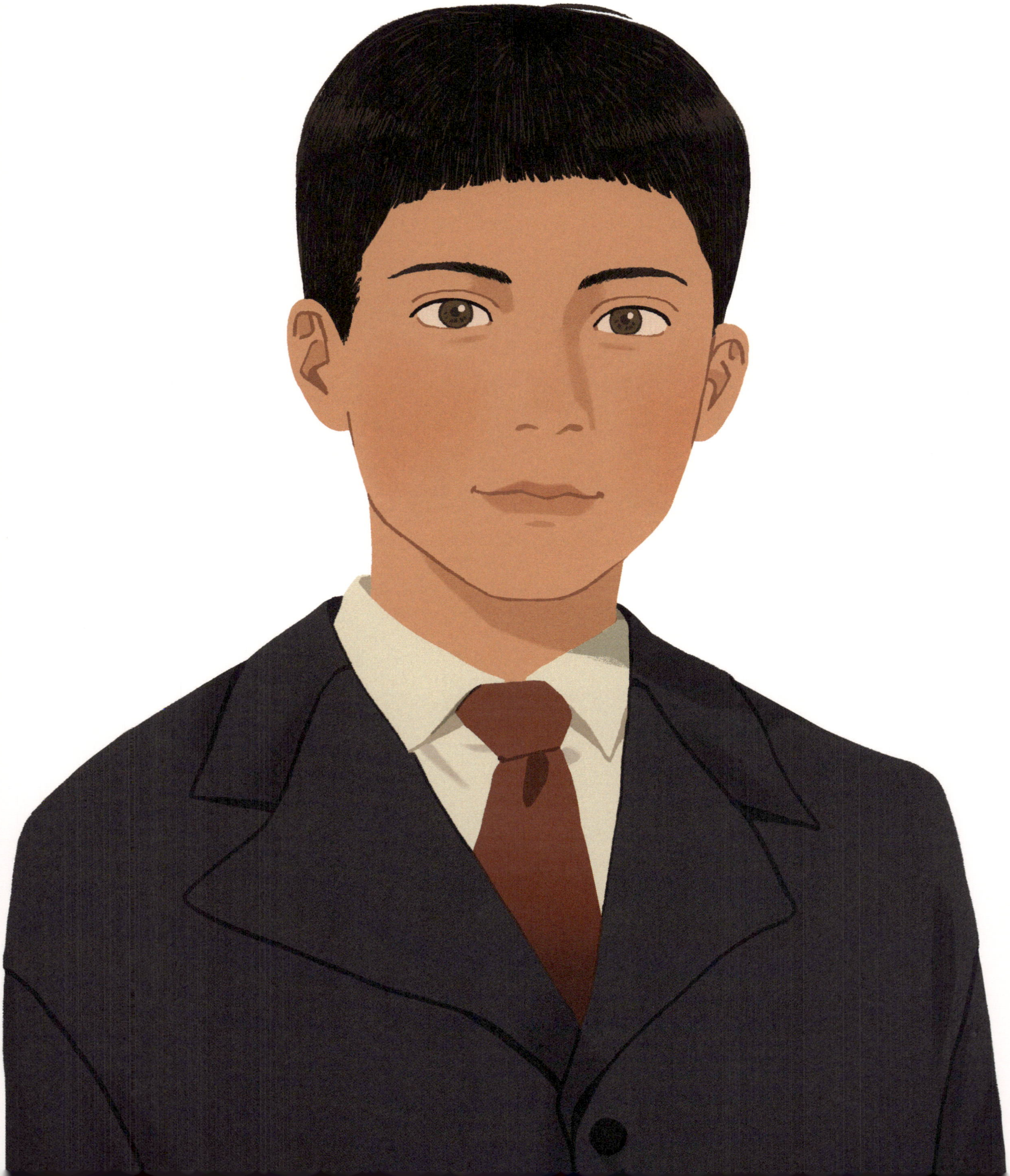

Saint José Luis Sanchez del Rio
(1913–1928)

1926. After the Mexican Revolution, the government had begun denying priests their civil rights. It was illegal for them to vote, publicly express their opinions, or even to wear clerics or a religious habit. Catholic education of children was banned. Freedom of worship was restricted, and monastic orders were suppressed. Priests and protesters who peacefully resisted the new laws were imprisoned or killed at an appalling rate. Finally, Mexican Catholics took up arms. In the city of Sahuayo, a boy of thirteen was following these events.

Wartime

The Sanchez del Rio family home resonated that morning with metallic clicking, loud voices, and impatient steps. José opened an eye, quickly got out of bed, and rushed to the living room. His older brothers, Miguel and Macario, were camped in front of the mirror, adjusting their military outfits: Macario his spurs, Miguel his pistol.

"Come on, it's time," their father said with controlled emotion. "Let's go."

He tried to hide his pain and anxiety. His wife was in tears.

"Take me with you," José begged, throwing his arms around Miguel.

His mother grabbed him.

"No, José, not you!" she exclaimed. "Thirteen is too young!"

"I want to serve Jesus!" José protested.

"You will serve him by staying at home and praying," his mother replied.

"We need your prayers, Josélito," Miguel added gently. "Mexico needs them."

I Can Cook the Beans!

1927. José Luis, pen in hand, was wondering how to conclude his letter. Suddenly, a mischievous smile appeared on his lips. Looking at the crucifix on the wall, he dipped the pen in the inkwell and finished his paragraph: "General, you might find me too young to fight, but I can cook beans like no one else, and I know some good jokes that will lift up the troops' morale."

A few weeks later, charmed by this unique letter, General Prudencio Mendoza accepted José Luis as a flag bearer. The teenager got to know the battlefields and life in the camps. The flying bullets, the smell of gunpowder, the whinnying horses, the cries of the wounded—in his ardor, he bore it all. Though he did not fight, he screamed the rallying cry of the Cristeros:[1] "Viva Cristo Rey!" Long live Christ the King!

He prayed for an end to the violence and injustice. How could anyone live happily in a country where the government tore down freedom of conscience and punished altar servers who rang bells at Mass, parents who taught their children to pray, and priests whose only crime was devoting their lives to God?

Take My Horse, General!

February 5, 1928. A gunshot. Sitting atop his horse, the valiant young flag bearer peered through the smoke and saw the general's horse suddenly collapse, the general tumble to the ground.

After a moment, General Mendoza stood up unscathed.

"Take my horse!" José yelled to him, jumping to the ground. "The Cristeros need you!"

Prudencio Mendoza had no time to refuse. José disappeared in the melee, leaving the horse. The general jumped in the saddle.

"Viva Cristo Rey!" he shouted, as he went back to fight.

Meanwhile, José struggled to escape the soldiers from the Federal Army who had rushed toward this easy prey. He was captured.

"I don't surrender," he said with bravado.

But there was no way he could fight these heavily armed men. They took him to the sacristy of the church in Sahuayo, which would be his prison.

We Will Meet Again

When José's father learned of his son's arrest, he offered a ransom to buy his freedom. His request was denied. The orders were implacable: eliminate all Cristeros without trial and without mercy. The boy was condemned to death.

When José heard his sentence, he wrote to his aunt to ask her to console his mother. Even these last letters were full of faith and inner strength. He had no regrets, except for making his mother cry.

The night before his execution, a great hope filled his heart. He penned these last words, later found in his pocket: "Dear Mama, they are going to kill me, but I want you to know that I am happy. Don't cry; we will meet again. José, who died for Christ the King."

---

1. See page 58.

February 10, 1928, 11:00 P.M. Sahuayo is asleep in the darkness of curfew. Suddenly...

¡Viva Cristo Rey, viva la Guadalupana!

That was Josélito's voice!

Impossible. He's locked up.

You, if you want to stay alive, shout "Death to Christ the King!"

¡Viva Cristo Rey!

These Federal monsters! They cut his feet to torture him!

José! I want to come with you!

Stay alive! You'll find other ways to serve Christ.

Say "Death to Christ the King" and we'll give you money to move to the United States.

But José Luis yelled "Viva Cristo Rey" one last time before being shot.

On October 16, 2016, Pope Francis canonized José Luis for his bravery in holding on to his faith.

JOSÉLITO, an Unarmed Soldier with a Valiant Heart

Surname: Sanchez del Rio
First name: José Luis (nickname: Josélito)
Born: March 28, 1913, in Sahuayo, Mexico
Died: February 10, 1928, in Sahuayo, Mexico
Parents: Macario Sanchez and Maria del Rio
Siblings: Three
Moments of weakness: Unknown
Moments of strength: Bravely witnessed to his faith in Christ even in grave danger
Patron of: Persecuted Christians, children, adolescents, and Sahuayo

Did You Know?

The number of Cristeros who fought at the peak of the revolt is estimated to be fifty thousand. Forty thousand were killed in combat, and many others were killed without trial after their capture.

ANOTHER MEXICAN MARTYR
Blessed Miguel Augustin Pro (1891–1927) joined the Jesuits at the age of twenty. In 1914, the first anticlerical laws forced him into exile in Belgium. Immediately after his ordination there in 1926, he returned to Mexico. Inventive and daring, he took on a variety of disguises in order to exercise his ministry and celebrate clandestine Masses. After a year, he and his two brothers were falsely accused of trying to kill a politician and given a death sentence. Just before he was put to death, Father Pro forgave his executioners. A photographer was there to document the punishment as an "example" to discourage the Cristeros, but the photo—which shows him stretching out his arms and shouting "Viva Cristo Rey!"—only heartened them! Miguel Pro was beatified in 1988 by Pope John Paul II.

PORFIRIO DIAZ AND THE "PORFIRIATO"
The Mexican Revolution and the subsequent political turmoil that led to the Cristeros' revolt found its origin in thirty years of dictatorship called the "Porfiriato." General Porfirio Diaz was pursuing a policy of rapid modernization of Mexico—one that enriched the wealthiest social classes at the cost of terrible inequalities, with most of the population remaining extremely poor. The revolution brought down this policy in 1911. However, despite their concern for social justice, the revolutionaries were blinded by their hatred of the Church, which they considered a force of oppression. Unjust and violent, the anti-Catholic government would inspire revolt.

Initially, "Cristeros" was a nickname used by their opponents to mock them since they used the word "Cristo"—Christ—so much. Rebels adopted the name with pride.

Timeline

- **1876–1911:** Dictatorship of Porfirio Diaz
- **1911:** Mexican Revolution begins.
- **March 28, 1913:** Birth of José Luis Sanchez del Rio
- **1917:** Mexico adopts an anti-Catholic constitution.
- **1924–1928:** Presidency of Plutarco Elias Calles, whose laws against Catholics lead to a revolt.
- **December 11, 1925:** Pope Pius XI writes an encyclical instituting the Feast of Christ the King.
- **November 23, 1927:** Martyrdom of Blessed Miguel Pro
- **February 1928:** Martyrdom of José Luis

Prayer to Saint José Luis Sanchez del Rio

Saint José,
inspire us with your courage and your joy,
as we need these every day
even if our hardships do not compare with yours.

Help us always to listen to our conscience
and not to compromise by doing what is wrong.

Help us to choose the good,
and to serve Christ, King of the Universe,
your friend, for whom you gave everything.

Pray for us, that we may have the desire
always to remain in Christ's friendship
and never let it go.
Amen.

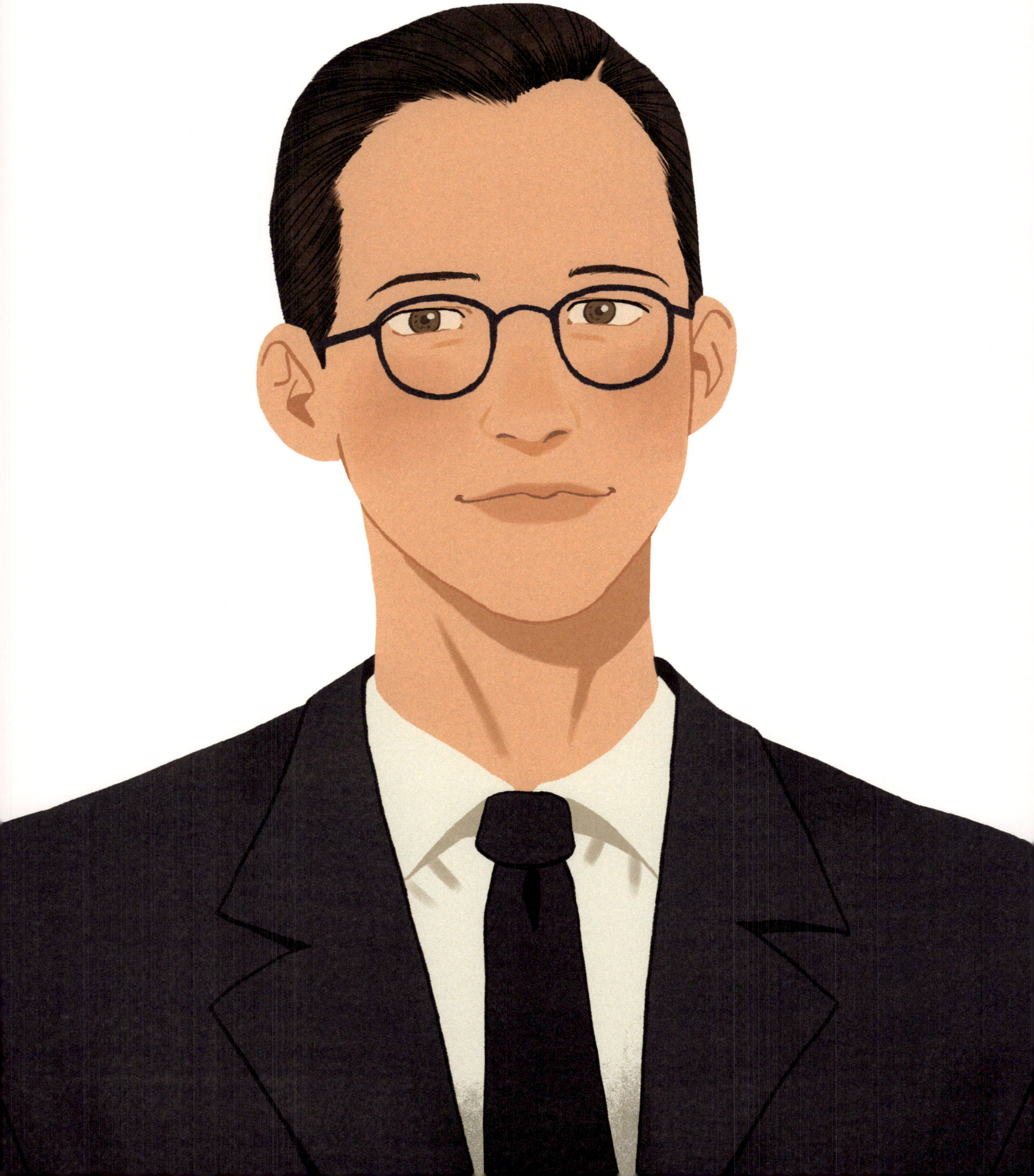

Blessed Marcel Callo
(1921–1945)

Holiness can flourish even in the heart of darkness. A young Frenchman, Marcel Callo, showed complete trust in God while imprisoned in Germany during the Second World War, under the ruthless Nazi dictatorship of Adolf Hitler.

A Twentieth-Century Knight

"Marcel Callo, what will your motto be?" the chaplain asked warmly.

The dark-haired child looked up at him and answered in a crystalline voice: "To pray, to receive Communion, to sacrifice myself, and to be an apostle!"

The priest nodded, moved by the seriousness of this little boy who was making his entrance today into the Eucharistic Crusade. In the 1920s, this youth movement trained children to be companions of Jesus—at his service and listening to him. Marcel was a promising rookie. The youngest in a family of nine children, he already had an ardent faith that he put into practice through many activities, especially the Scouts. To be an apostle? It suited him perfectly. He experienced the certainty of Jesus' love for all men, and he wanted to spread this Good News, to make people free and happy.

Welcome to the YCW

"You want to join the YCW? You? Do you already have a job?"

The head of the Young Christian Workers organization in Rennes looked amused at this frail kid with glasses—such a young face with a sparkling smile.

"Yes, I do," Marcel replied. "I have been an apprentice in a typography workshop since I was twelve years old."

"Ah! Good. And you know the rules of the YCW?"

"Of course: to put prayer at the center of all action, at work and at home.

"In that case, welcome aboard, Marcel. We're happy to have you!"

That was the start of Marcel's tremendous spiritual journey. His spiritual growth was in line with his childhood promise: to pray, to receive Communion, to sacrifice himself, to be an apostle. Both at the workshop and at home, he strove daily to be a disciple of Jesus.

At the YCW, the Lord placed someone in his path: Marguerite. She lived with the same Christian zeal. They fell in love and got engaged.

Forbidden to Be an Apostle

June 1940. France was conquered, and German troops arrived in Brittany, in the north. The Nazi occupiers forbade all kinds of freedoms, stifling any opposition to Hitler's rule. Christians were dangerous in their view, because Christians had only one master—and it was not Adolph Hitler. The Nazis suppressed all Catholic organizations, including the YCW. This did not intimidate Marcel and Marguerite, who remained more faithful than ever to Jesus Christ. Marcel continued to talk to others about Jesus, with laughter in his eyes, radiating his joy in Christ even in the gloomiest circumstances. He participated in clandestine, that is, secret, meetings with his fellow Jocists.[1] The promise "to be an apostle" became more important and urgent than ever under the Nazi rule.

Missionary in the Third Reich

March 19, 1943. Marcel and Marguerite traveled through Rennes; the city was devastated. Ten days earlier, the area had been bombed, and Marie-Madeleine, one of Marcel's sisters, had been killed. They were terribly sad. And to make things worse, Marcel was now being forced to leave for Germany to join the labor forces. In the train station, Marcel tried to console his fiancée: "I'm going there as a missionary, Marguerite. Germans need to hear about Christ. And I'll be back as soon as my tour is over. We will get married! Have faith."

---

1. A "Jocist" is a member of the Jeunesse Ouvrière Chrétienne, the Young Christian Workers.

Autumn 1943. Marcel is forced to work in a weapons factory.

"We'll be eating some bread tonight."
"Great!"
"Silence!"

The bread is the Eucharist. Marcel attends secret Masses whenever he can.

"I've never believed in God, Marcel, but you make me think..."
"Me too. I liked this secret meeting with the Jocists."

Marcel's goal is to provide comfort and moral support.

"Stop them! These catholics are enemies of the state."

The contagious faith of Marcel and his comrades infuriates the Nazis.

"... as we forgive those who trespass against us ..."

Marcel and eleven friends are locked up in prison. They pray there in front of a cross made of flowers.

My Dear Marguerite, Tomorrow I'll be taken to a work camp. But with Jesus, everything is possible. Let's not give up. Mar...

Marcel died of exhaustion at the concentration camp of Mauthausen, in March 1945. Christian, missionary, and brave until the end.

MARCEL, Witness to Jesus in the Darkness

Surname: Callo
First name: Marcel
Born: December 6, 1921, in Rennes, France
Died: March 19, 1945, in Mauthausen, Austria
Parents: Jean Callo and Felicite Callo
Siblings: Eight
Occupation: Typographer
Moments of weakness: Unknown
Moments of strength: Risked his life in a work camp; told others about Jesus
Patron of: Young men and women who seek to live Christian lives as laypersons

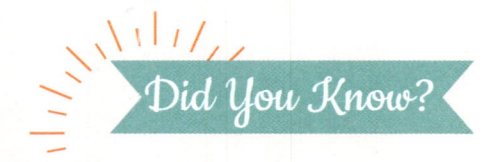

☞ **THE STO[1] (COMPULSORY WORK SERVICE)** was established in February 1943 by the French Vichy government, at the demand of the Germans after they had invaded France. The Compulsory Work Service forced French people age twenty-one to twenty-three, as well as women over twenty-five without children, to work in German factories or farms for two years, to compensate for the Germans' lack of manpower during the war. About 650,000 French people were forcibly transferred to Germany. Another 200,000 chose to disobey the law and joined the French Resistance. Marcel Callo obeyed the STO to avoid reprisals against his family, and with the firm intention of being a missionary there among the workers.

---
1. STO stands for *Service du travail obligatoire*.

Did You Know?

JOC, JAC, JEC
Founded in Belgium by Father Joseph Cardijn in 1925 and brought to France in 1927 by Father Georges Guérin, JOC was a youth movement for working-class people. To join a section of the JOC meant to live one's faith in the working world, which was already largely de-Christianized at the time of Marcel Callo. In 1940, the JOC had approximately 85,000 members. Two other similar associations existed for other circles: the JAC (Catholic Agricultural Youth) and the JEC (Christian Student Youth). These three associations went underground in 1940 and contributed to the French Resistance.

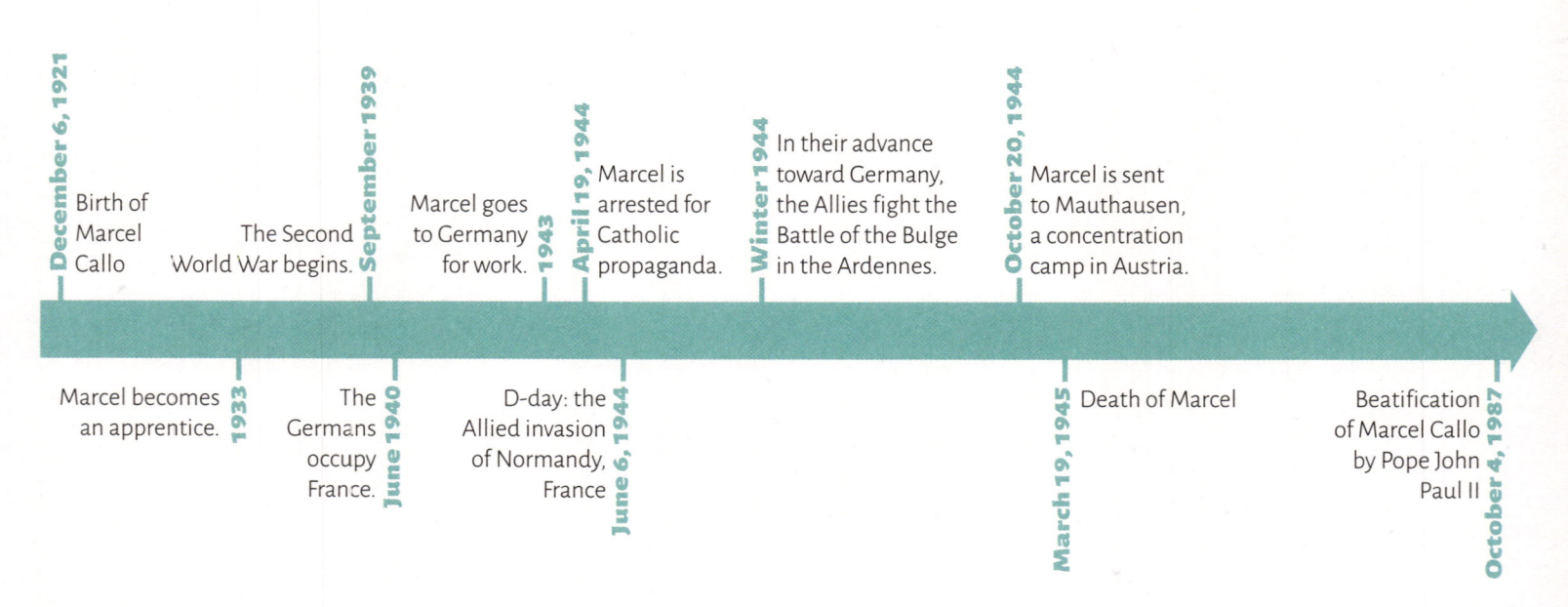

Timeline

- **December 6, 1921:** Birth of Marcel Callo
- **1933:** Marcel becomes an apprentice.
- **September 1939:** The Second World War begins.
- **June 1940:** The Germans occupy France.
- **1943:** Marcel goes to Germany for work.
- **April 19, 1944:** Marcel is arrested for Catholic propaganda.
- **June 6, 1944:** D-day: the Allied invasion of Normandy, France
- **Winter 1944:** In their advance toward Germany, the Allies fight the Battle of the Bulge in the Ardennes.
- **October 20, 1944:** Marcel is sent to Mauthausen, a concentration camp in Austria.
- **March 19, 1945:** Death of Marcel
- **October 4, 1987:** Beatification of Marcel Callo by Pope John Paul II

Prayer to Blessed Marcel Callo

Blessed Marcel,
help us, like you, to have an ardent soul,
dedicated to serving Jesus.
Help us to live as missionaries
in all circumstances of our lives.

You have known sadness, exhaustion,
hunger, cold, and hostility in a foreign land;
and yet these hardships did not bring you down,
because you placed your hope in Jesus,
conqueror of darkness and evil.

Help us in times of fatigue and discouragement;
remind us that the light keeps on shining
thanks to Jesus Christ, our Lord and Savior.
Amen.

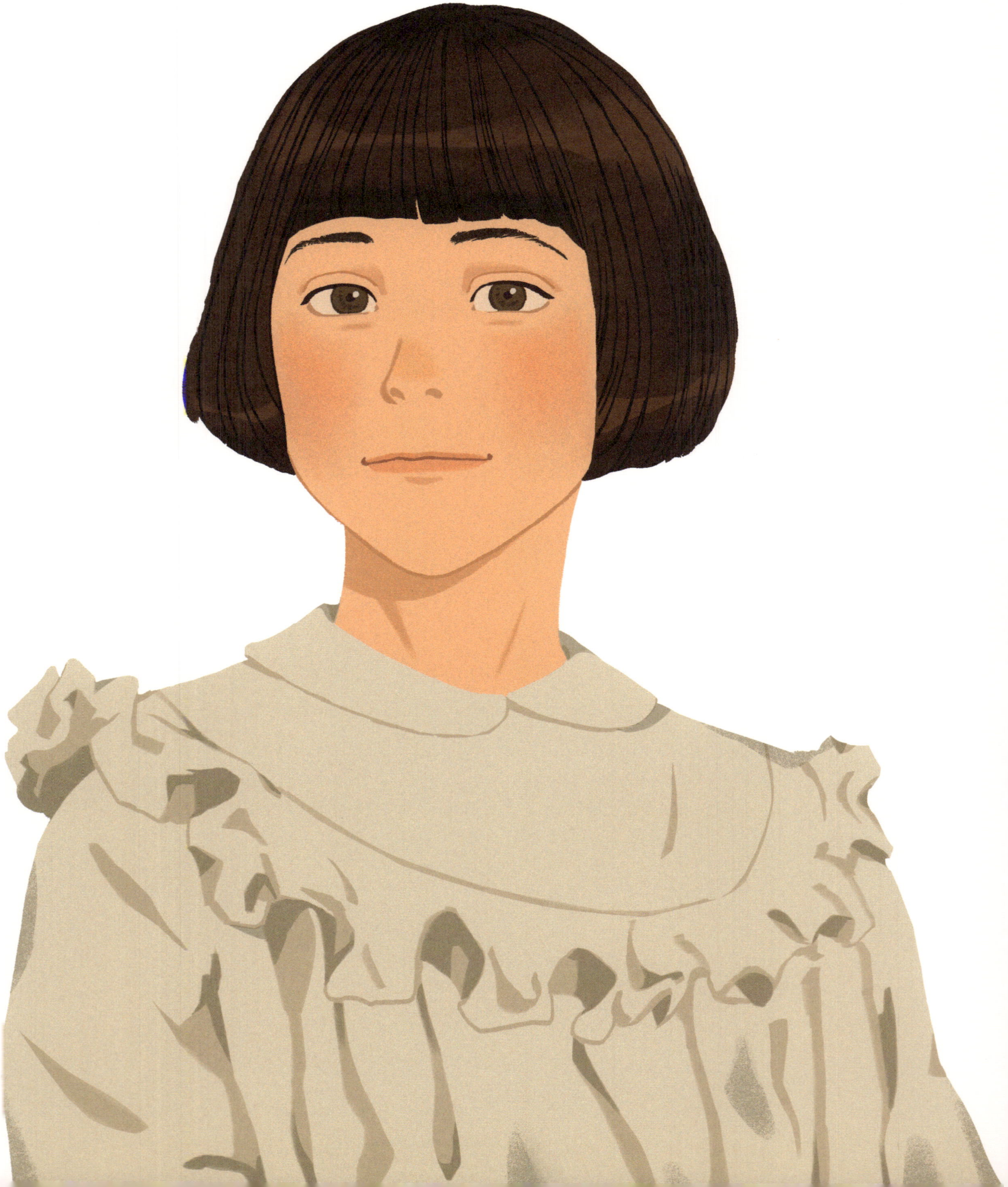

Venerable Antonietta Meo
(1930–1937)

In photos, Antonietta—nicknamed Nennolina by her parents—seems like so many young girls her age: a bobbed haircut and a sparkling gaze, full of life. Yet she was different from most. Before her death at age seven, she wrote more than 150 letters to Jesus and to the Blessed Virgin!

Funny and Brave

On the morning of September 15, 1936, rays of sunlight fell upon the gentle face of Nennolina, seated by the window. Her gaze roamed over the street, flew over the rooftops, and stopped at the façade of the Basilica of the Holy Cross. Antonietta Meo was taking a mental stroll through her neighborhood in Rome, where she had lived with her parents and her sister Margherita since her birth almost six years ago.

Familiar footsteps made the floor creak behind her.

"Hi, Nennolina!" her mother called out. "Can I help you put on your prosthesis?"

The little girl swiveled her wheelchair. This past April, she had lost her left leg due to bone cancer. Despite the discomfort of the prosthesis that replaced it, she quickly got up, once her mother finished securing it in place.

"I was thinking of something while looking at the church, Mama."

"What were you thinking about, Nennolina?"

"Well, I want to make my First Communion."

"It's funny," Mrs. Meo replied with a smile, "I was just going to suggest that you write to the sisters to ask them if you could. They might allow you to prepare to receive it at Christmas."

"Yes!" Antonietta exclaimed. "And there's another letter I want to write too."

How to Mail a Letter to Jesus?

A half hour later, several papers were spread out on the table and quivering in a light breeze. Antonietta didn't know how to write yet, but she dictated her messages to her mother.

"Let's recap," Mrs. Meo said with a mischievous smile. "I already put your letter to the sisters in an envelope and addressed it. But the one you wrote to Jesus, I'm not so sure where to send it!"

"You can put it under the statue of the baby Jesus in the church. He will come and read it."

Mrs. Meo complied.

As the weeks went by, Antonietta dictated dozens and dozens of letters, sometimes written to Jesus and sometimes to his mother, the Blessed Virgin Mary.

A Little Word of Love

Walking with the prosthesis was often painful, yet Nennolina did not complain. Instead, she offered her suffering to Jesus, saying, "May each step I take be a little word of love."

Months passed, and the cancer kept spreading. The little girl never complained of any pain. One day, her mother asked the doctor, "Is my daughter suffering at all?"

"With this disease, yes, of course! It is excruciating!"

Sensing that her daughter must be receiving grace from God to overcome the pain, she went to the child and asked, "Nennolina, will you bless me—bless Mama?"

First Communion

December 24, 1936. As the Church was celebrating the birth of Jesus all over the world, Antonietta was ready to receive Jesus in her heart with an immense fervor. Her parents, her sister, her friends from church, and the nuns who had taught her the catechism were all gathered around her. That night, she hardly suffered. Her soul was overflowing with joy. After taking Communion, she stayed on her knees for more than an hour, her hands joined in prayer.

Antonietta's Letter Reaches the Pope

June 2, 1937. Antonietta dictated a new letter to her mother, with difficulty.

> Dear Jesus the Crucified,
>
> I love you so much. I want to stay with you on Calvary, and I suffer with joy because I know I'm on Calvary. Dear Jesus, I thank you for having sent me this illness because it is a means to get to Paradise. Dear Jesus, tell God the Father that I love Him too. . . Dear Jesus, give me the strength to bear this pain that I offer for sinners.

Overwhelmed, her mother crumpled up the letter and threw it into a drawer.

A few days later, at the request of the Meos' family doctor, the pope's doctor came to visit the little girl and talked with her for a long time.

"Your child is extraordinary," he said to Mrs. Meo.

"Yes. And if you only knew how many letters she has written to Jesus and Mary!"

Mrs. Meo handed him the most recent one, all wrinkled.

As the doctor read it, he eyes welled with tears.

"May I show it to the Holy Father?" he asked.

That same afternoon, Pope Pius XI read the letter. But he knew that it was intended for someone even more important: Jesus.

"I am sent by His Holiness the Pope to bless your daughter."

"His Holiness and his physician ask you to pray for them, Antonietta."

"When you're healed, we'll take you to the sea."

"Don't worry, Mama. In about ten days, I'll be out of this bed."

"Bless me, Nennolina."

"Do you want to receive the holy oils, Antonietta? They will give you more strength."

"Oh yes! I do!"

Mrs. Meo doesn't understand that Antonietta has given her the date of her departure to heaven.

"The Lord be with you, now and always."

"They say that the first word your daughter knew how to pronounce was 'Jesus.'"

"Not at all! It was 'Mama,' like everyone else!"

Antonietta surrendered her soul to God at dawn on July 3, with her parents at her side, after pronouncing these last words with a smile: "Jesus, Mary, Mama, Papa."

The name of Antonietta remains well-known in the Vatican, because an investigation is underway to proclaim her Blessed Antonietta—worthy of inspiring children everywhere.

69

NENNOLINA, *Letters for Heaven's Mailbox*

Surname: Meo
First name: Antonietta (nickname: Nennolina)
Born: December 15, 1930, in Rome, Italy
Died: July 3, 1937, in Rome, Italy
Parents: Michele Meo and Maria Ravaglioli
Siblings: Three (two eldest in heaven, then Margherita)

Pius XI (1857–1939)
A Pope Concerned for the World

A scholar as well as an athlete, Pius XI maintained, from his mountaineer youth, great tenacity in the face of hardship. He was able to stay firm in the 1930s, an era dominated by Fascism, Nazism, and Communism. He published encyclicals condemning these ideologies. Learning that Hitler was planning to visit Rome on May 3, 1938, he left the Vatican with all his staff on April 30. He asked that no lights be turned on throughout the week of Hitler's visit and that all Vatican museums remain closed, so that the Führer could not visit them. To show his displeasure with the dictator Mussolini, Pope Pius XI left Rome for six months and stayed at his residence of Castel Gandolfo, the longest stay outside Rome for a pope in centuries.

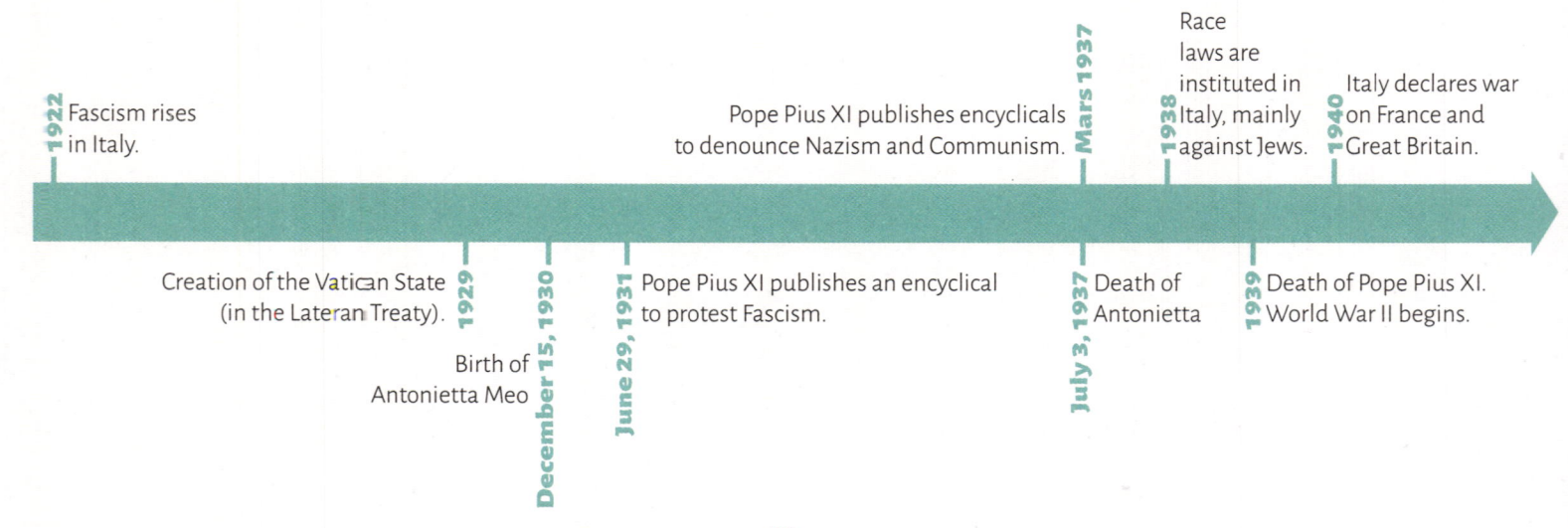

Did You Know?

Catholic Action in Italy

Catholic Action was an important Church movement launched in 1905. It brought together about two million members, including many children divided by age groups. Antonietta was part of the "Piccolissime" for toddlers. Then, when a bit older, part of the "Beniamine." Catholic Action was opposed to the Fascist dictator Mussolini, who sought to recruit young Italians in his Balilla movement (similar to the Hitler Youth in Germany). In 1937, Mussolini banned the Scouts and other youth associations. However, the firm reaction of Pope Pius XI held him back from dissolving Catholic Action.

☞ **BONE CANCER: WHAT IS IT?** Cancer is the multiplication of abnormal cells. There are several types of bone cancer, and Antonietta's was osteosarcoma. Although osteosarcoma remains very serious today, it can now be treated with a much greater chance of success than was possible in Antonietta's time.

Timeline:

- **1922** Fascism rises in Italy.
- **1929** Creation of the Vatican State (in the Lateran Treaty).
- **December 15, 1930** Birth of Antonietta Meo
- **June 29, 1931** Pope Pius XI publishes an encyclical to protest Fascism.
- **Mars 1937** Pope Pius XI publishes encyclicals to denounce Nazism and Communism.
- **July 3, 1937** Death of Antonietta
- **1938** Race laws are instituted in Italy, mainly against Jews.
- **1939** Death of Pope Pius XI. World War II begins.
- **1940** Italy declares war on France and Great Britain.

Prayer to Antonietta Meo

Venerable Antonietta,
you who often wrote to Jesus and Mary,
we reach out to you,
now that you are in heaven
and we are on earth.

By your example, you showed us
that we can address heaven very simply,
in the words of a child,
and that we will be heard and understood,
our prayers answered.

Help us to remain faithful,
praying to God with love and simplicity,
even when we grow up.

You who prayed so much for others,
inspire us with your generosity.
Help us to keep our hearts
attentive to the needs of others,
a prayerful companion in their joys and their sorrows.
Amen.

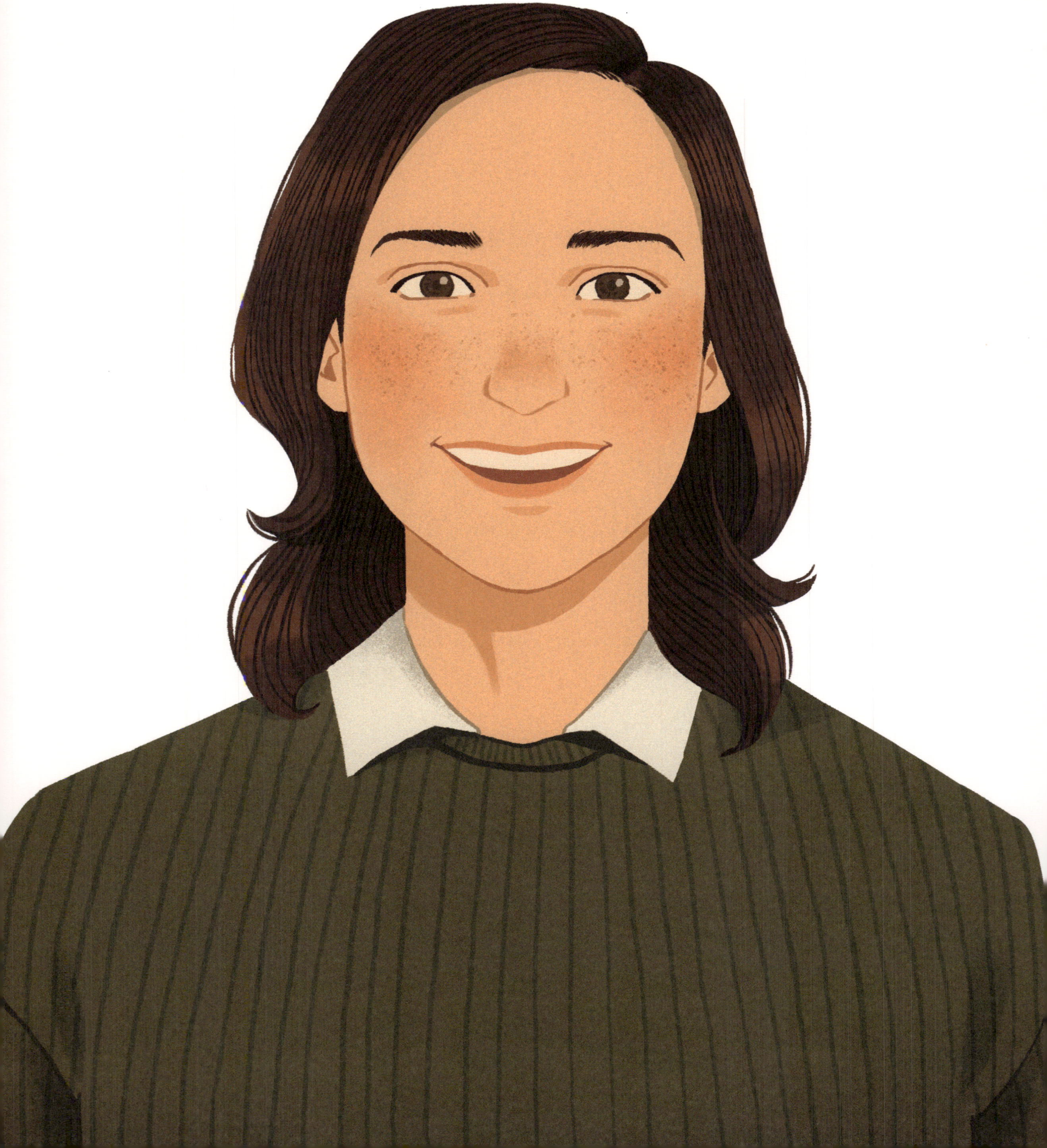

Claire de Castelbajac
(1953–1975)

Some first names are particularly suited to the people who bear them. Claire de Castelbajac well deserved hers. In French, claire *means "bright, clear," and from very early in her life, Claire was sensitive to the light of God, to his goodness, and to the happiness he brings. "Joy" was perhaps her favorite word. Here is the story of this young girl with a radiant soul.*

Ambition for the Future
"Father, guess what I want to be when I grow up."

Mr. de Castelbajac looked up from his newspaper and smiled. Eight-year-old Claire was waiting for his answer, standing with a mischievous look on her pale face. Since her earliest childhood, she had often been sick, sometimes with serious illnesses including toxicosis, pulmonary congestion, diphtheria, and intestinal infection, but her fragile health never discouraged her from living her life fully, in peace and trust.

"Hmm," her father replied. "I think I have an idea. A religious sister, perhaps?"

Claire shook her head.

"Oh no! I want to be a saint. It's even better than a sister!"

Too Much Happiness
Claire was full of joy—a joy rooted in her deep faith.

"Mama, I feel so much happiness; it's overflowing. Do you want me to give some to you? I am happy, happy, full of happiness—a happiness that cannot be defined!"

Claire did not have a typical childhood. Too sick to go to class, she was homeschooled. She was often in pain and could have complained, the way most of us do. But she did not.

At age twelve, she was finally able to attend school. Since her family lived in a small village without many resources for education, she went to boarding school in Toulouse, France, and stayed in that city until college. The extraordinary beauty of Toulouse moved Claire so much that she decided to study art restoration, learning to bring old works of art back to life. After passing a difficult test, she moved to Rome and entered a prestigious school.

In the Whirlwind of Rome

1972. Claire was now in Rome. In the bustle of the Italian capital—with its parties, its noise, and its handsome boys—Claire felt confused. Everything here was so different from the life she knew! She lived in a whirlwind of outings and distractions. It was not always easy to find room for prayer or for good works. Following her friends' example, Claire gradually became more interested in parties than in Christ, and she even began to doubt her faith. But with this, she also felt her joy disappearing. Even her studies suffered from lack of effort during this time. Her professors warned that she could be dismissed if her behavior didn't change.

But God was there watching over her. In September 1974, Claire took the opportunity to make a pilgrimage to the Holy Land, to the places where Jesus had lived. There she reconnected with the Lord and, immediately, with a deep sense of happiness.

"Here in the Holy Land, I see the love of God, huge, amazing, and so simple."

If heaven is the praise of God, I am already there.

October 1974. Claire is sent to restore frescoes in Assisi.

Beauty, joy, and praise fill her daily life.

Christmas holidays in France. On December 30, in Lourdes, Claire falls deep in prayer. A few days later, she is diagnosed with meningitis.

I need to praise him.

Claire said she wanted to spread joy everywhere around her: it was the project of her life.

It's still happening: here her joy shines on!

... where many vocations have come thanks to her intercession. You can pray in the chapel dedicated to her.

Claire, inspire us with your joy—in our faith and in our lives.

These are Claire's last words.

Claire rests at Boulaur Abbey outside Toulouse...

CLAIRE, a Deep Sense of Joy

Surname: de Castelbajac
First name: Claire
Born: October 26, 1953, in Paris, France
Died: January 22, 1975, in Toulouse, France
Parents: Louis de Castelbajac and Solange de Castelbajac
Siblings: Four (all elder, from her father's first marriage)
Moment of weakness: Period of doubt and superficiality in Rome during her studies
Moments of strength: Rediscovering her faith and her love of God

Did You Know?

A Difficult Contest
The prestigious Central Institute of Restoration, in Rome, offered only three spots every year to international students who could pass the test. Claire was selected, proof of her intelligence and hard work.

☞ **CLAIRE AND THE MONASTERY OF BOULAUR** In 1979, the Cistercian nuns of the Abbey of Boulaur, located more than fifteen miles from where Claire lived, faced an uncertain future. There were only five sisters, and their community would have to close if they did not find more vocations. A Cistercian abbot in charge suggested that they pray to Claire de Castelbajac, who, in his eyes, could be beatified if she accomplished a miracle. They had to ask her for five new religious vocations. The sisters were skeptical, but they began to pray, and within the year, five new postulants arrived!

☞ **I'M FED UP!** Although Claire had a lively and luminous faith, not everything was easy for her! In 1971, in a letter to her sister written at a time when their mother was ill, she wrote: "I'm fed up... so fed up." Episodes of fatigue and poor health kept affecting her family, especially Claire. She had to face hardship and pain, and she did so with admirable courage.

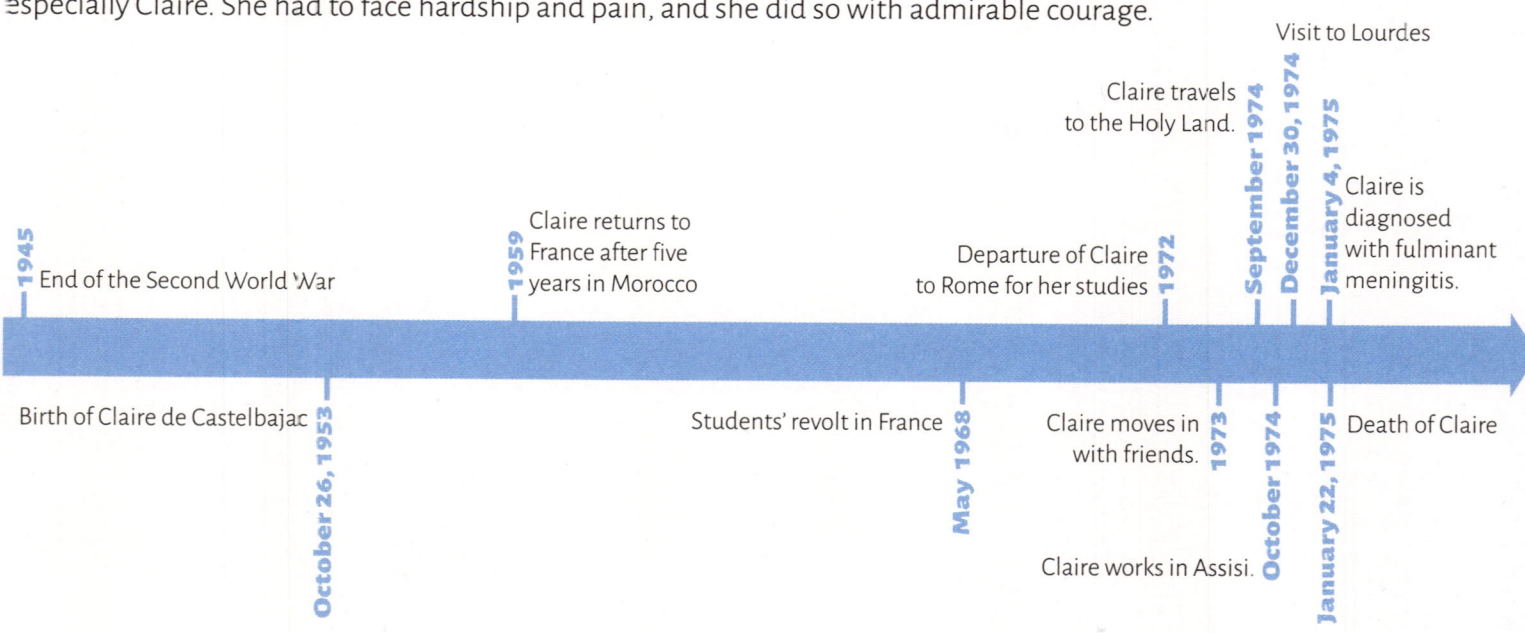

Timeline:

- 1945 — End of the Second World War
- October 26, 1953 — Birth of Claire de Castelbajac
- 1959 — Claire returns to France after five years in Morocco
- May 1968 — Students' revolt in France
- 1972 — Departure of Claire to Rome for her studies
- 1973 — Claire moves in with friends.
- September 1974 — Claire travels to the Holy Land.
- October 1974 — Claire works in Assisi.
- December 30, 1974 — Visit to Lourdes
- January 4, 1975 — Claire is diagnosed with fulminant meningitis.
- January 22, 1975 — Death of Claire

Prayer to Claire de Castelbajac

Servant of God Claire,
you who wanted to sow joy around you,
inspire us with the same desire
to make God known to others
with our radiant joy.

From heaven, look upon our world
where there is so much sadness and pain.
Pray for all people who don't yet believe,
and ask the Lord to instill trust,
hope, and deep joy
in the hearts of all his children.
Amen.

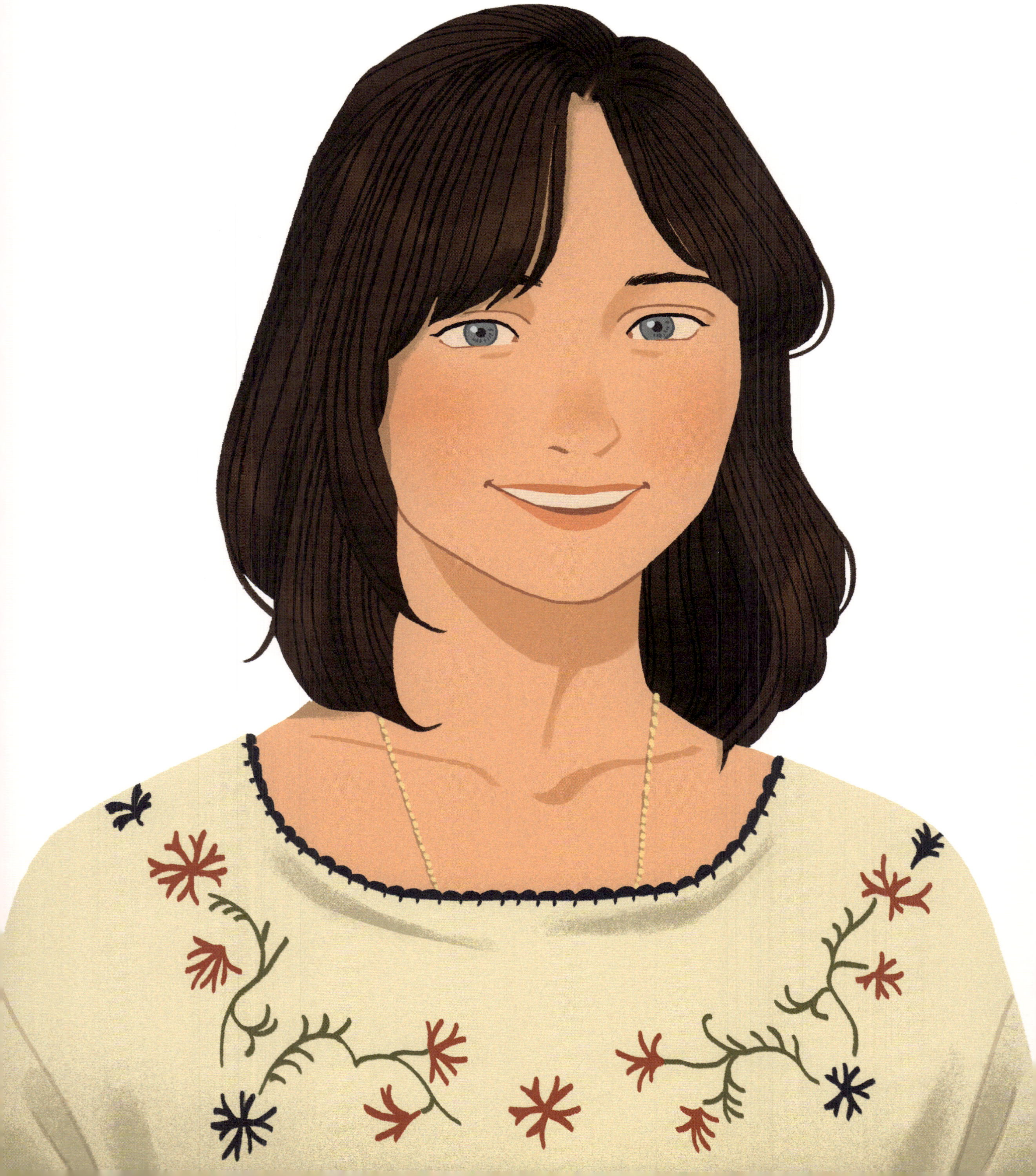

Blessed Sandra Sabattini

(1961–1984)

"You shall love the Lord, and with all your soul, and with all your strength, and with all your mind; and your neighbor as yourself" (Luke 10:27). Sandra's whole life—her activities, her studies, her projects—was placed under the banner of these two commandments, which Jesus said were the greatest.

A Decisive Meeting

On a fine day in 1974, Father Oreste Benzi was giving a lecture. For the hundredth time, the Italian priest was presenting the work he had founded six years ago, the Community of Pope John XXIII. The community helps all people in distress, whether through disabilities, poverty, or addiction.

"There are many problems, but with charity and good will, we can do anything," Father Benzi concluded.

While a basket was passed around to raise funds to help disadvantaged children spend time in the mountains, the priest saw a little girl approaching him. He had already noticed her, and not just because of her bright red sweater. She had been listening intently to his every word.

"Hi, Father. My name is Sandra Sabattini."

"Hello, Sandra. Are you from Rimini?"

"Not too far," she explained. "I live in Misano Adriatico with my family, at my uncle's; he is a priest. I would like to serve in your community."

"How old are you?" Father Benzi asked, surprised.

"I'm twelve," Sandra answered.

"You are very young!" the priest exclaimed.

"Is that a problem?" Sandra asked.

"Certainly not," he replied, amused.

"We Broke Our Bones"

Summer 1975. Sandra's bedroom was filled with the joyous jumble of a return from camp: clothes to be sorted, a down jacket to air out, walking shoes drying on the window ledge. Sandra pulled out of her bag her diary—her daily companion since she was ten years old. At this camp in the mountains, where she was a counselor to children with disabilities, she had hardly had time to write. Now, sitting at her desk, she summarized her trip, which had been tiring but very intense: "We broke our bones, but they are people I will never give up on." The teenager had just found her way in life, even if she didn't know it yet. From then on, she would commit to helping the most vulnerable.

A Radiant Student

October 1980. At the entrance of the prestigious medical school at the University of Bologna, a sweet brunette caught the eye of a few boys. Not only she was pretty, she was radiant! And when she smiled, she had stars in her eyes!

"Forget it, guys," a young man whispered to his friends that morning. "Guess where she starts her days? At the church. Half an hour of silent prayer each morning before she comes to class!"

Sandra kindly greeted her admirers and went on her way.

"How do you know?" a boy whispered to the gossiper. "Did she tell you?"

"No! I just followed her in there out of curiosity, since we take the same route to school. But I'll stop before I turn into a church lady!"

The boys burst out laughing as they watched Sandra chatting with friends. They had to recognize that her faith did not make her austere or distant. What charm, what zest for life!

Fiancée, Full of Ideas

Spring 1984. A young couple walked along the beach in Rimini. Her eyes fixed on the horizon, Sandra had a thousand ideas for her future with Guido. She had met him within the Community of Pope John XXIII. They fell in love with each other and got engaged. Sandra dreamed of becoming a missionary doctor in Africa; Guido was ready to follow her. And if that wasn't possible, then they would dedicate themselves to the service of vulnerable people in Italy.

"Did you write something in your notebook yesterday?" Guido asked.

In her diary, Sandra wrote down her spiritual thoughts day by day, and she liked to share them with her fiancé.

"Yes. I wrote that nothing in my life is mine. I need to remember that at all time. Everything is given to us, right, Guido? We have to take care of this gift. We have to make it rich and beautiful for the day God comes."

Sandra always started her day with a prayer.

She continued her medical studies...

"Your blood pressure is improving!"

"Thanks!"

...and kept volunteering too.

"Sandra, tell me another story!"

"Another one? That will make six!"

"Life is tough, my dear."

"You are not alone, Franca."

Sandra accompanied people facing the worst...

"The world is so beautiful."

... while keeping an incredible capacity for wonder.

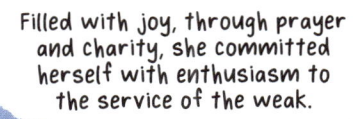

"How can Sandra manage to stay so cheerful?"

"Hmm. Her friendship with God helps."

"I saw everything. The girl was hit."

On April 29, 1984, Sandra was hit by a car. She succumbed to her wounds three days later.

Sandra's life was fulfilled. She gave so much. She is now among the saints.

Filled with joy, through prayer and charity, she committed herself with enthusiasm to the service of the weak.

In 2021, Pope Francis announced Sandra's beatification.

SANDRA, Generosity in Action

Surname: Sabattini
First name: Sandra
Born: August 19, 1961, in Rimini, Italy
Died: May 2, 1984, in Bologna, Italy
Parents: Giuseppe Sabattini and Agnese Bonini
Siblings: One (Raffaele)
Occupation: Medical student
Moment of weakness: Unknown
Moment of strength: Daily devotion to prayer

The following quotes are taken from Sandra's diary:

"The goal of my life is to unite with the Lord; the tool to achieve this is prayer."

"Thank you, Lord, because I have received beautiful things from my present life; I have everything, but above all I thank you because you have revealed yourself to me, because I have been able to know you."

"If I truly love, how can I accept to see a third of the people in the world starve to death? While I stay safe and comfortable? If I did that, maybe I would be a good Christian, but not holy! Today, there is an increase of good Christians, when the world needs saints!"

Did You Know?

Father Oreste Benzi (1925–2007)
Who was this priest who made such an impact on Sandra?

The son of a worker and seventh in a family of nine children, Oreste Benzi entered the minor seminary as a teenager and was ordained in 1949, at the age of twenty-four. Beside his responsibilities as a teacher in the seminary and a parish priest, he centered his life around helping the disadvantaged, even if—especially if—they were not Catholics. Affable and cheerful, sensitive to the most diverse forms of distress, he founded the Community of Pope John XXIII to serve Jesus Christ by serving the poor. His influence was important. A case for beatification has been opened to recognize him as a Servant of God.

☞ "**SANDRA** had an intense relationship with God. She lived every moment with deep joy. She enjoyed the entire universe, discovering with him all its beauties. She lived tending toward the Infinite, Light, Mystery, Love."

—Father Oreste Benzi

August 19, 1961 — Birth of Sandra Sabattini
Engagement to Guido Rossi
1979
1980 — Sandra begins her medical studies.
October 16, 1978 — Election of Pope John Paul II
May 2, 1984 — Death of Sandra
October 24, 2021 — Beatification of Sandra by Pope Francis

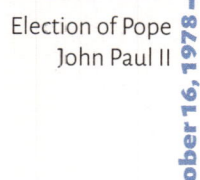

Prayer to Blessed Sandra Sabattini

Blessed Sandra,
you were a model of faith and joy
to everyone around you:
to those who knew you well,
to strangers who crossed your path,
to those who were in good health,
and to those who were weak or vulnerable.

Help us to be like you
in our daily lives.
Help us to believe the gospel wholeheartedly
and to serve Jesus Christ in all simplicity
in our behavior, our actions, and our laughter.
Help us to maintain a devoted prayer life,
to build our lives on the rock of God's love.
Amen.

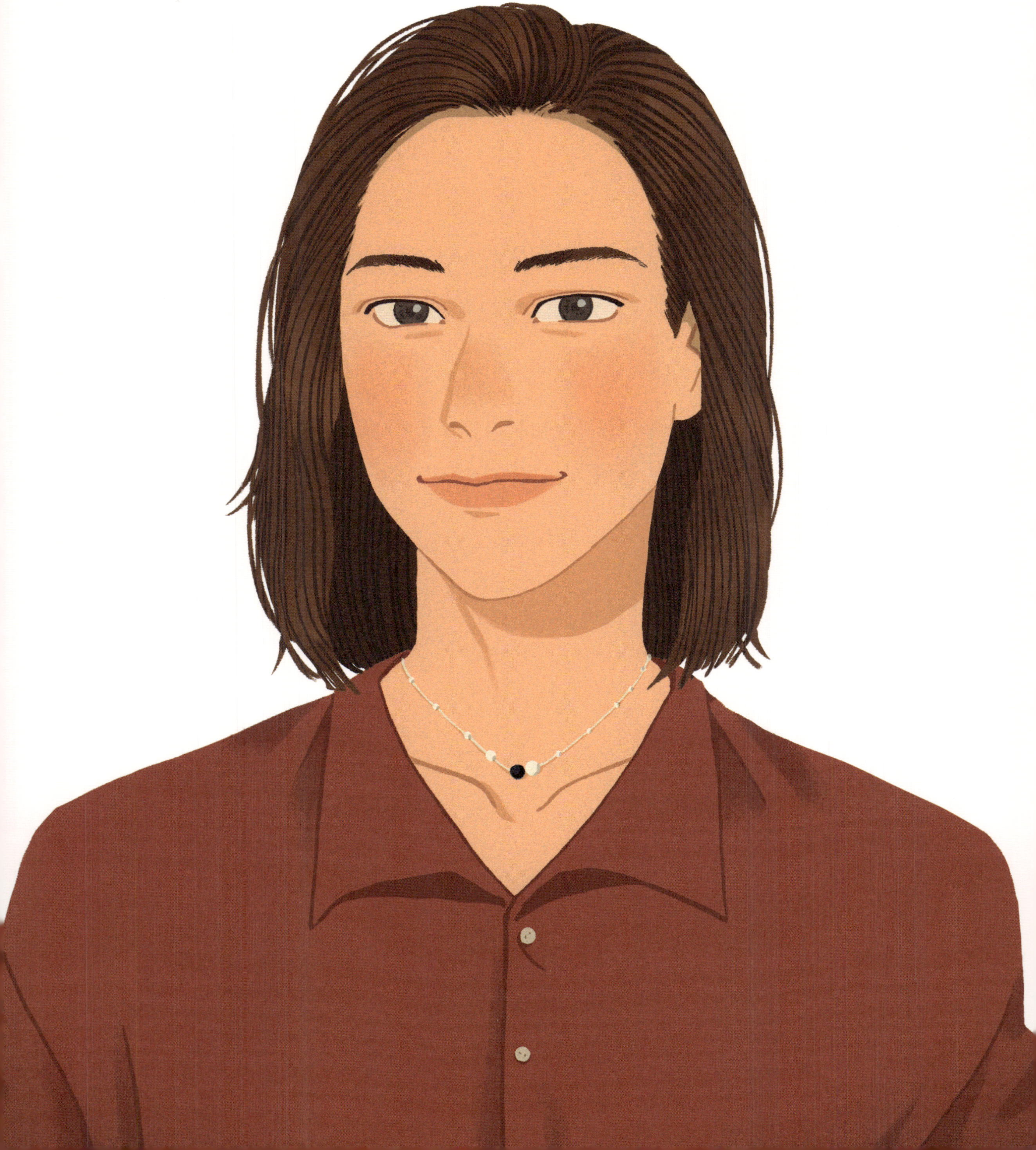

Blessed Chiara Badano
(1971–1990)

Her name was Chiara Badano, better known by the nickname she received a few months before she was called to God: Chiara Luce, which means "clear light" in Italian. What did Blessed Chiara Luce teach us? She taught us that every part of life can bear fruit, even through sickness, death, and beyond.

Five Years Old, and a Character

Maria Teresa Badano chuckled as she peeked into Chiara's room. The five-year-old girl was playing on the floor in the middle of scattered toys. This cheerful mess warmed her mother's heart.

For eleven years, Maria Teresa and her husband had hoped for this mess—for a child. Chiara was a gift from God, and she was making them so happy!

From the kitchen, the mother called for her daughter: "Chiaretta, how about we pray together? Just a short prayer."

"No, I don't pray."

Maria Teresa smiled at the frank and direct answer, so true to her daughter's assertive temperament.

"Good, good, as you wish! In that case, I will pray for both of us."

Mrs. Badano began to say the Our Father aloud, but almost immediately, she had to stifle a laugh. A small voice had joined her. Chiara had changed her mind!

An Immense Love of God

Chiara's eyes and ears were not yet big enough to capture all the energy that surrounded her. Hundreds of other children gathered around her to sing their joy over God's goodness. She was nine years old, and her parents had taken her to a national meeting of the Focolare Movement. The goal of this Christian group, composed mainly of lay people, is to let the love of God shine in daily life. This first gathering, in 1980, was a revelation to Chiara, and it would fill her life with the certainty that God was present at all times of the day.

Chiara's Secret

June 1985. Two girls were chatting in the sun, sitting on the beach in Savona, Italy.

"What's your secret? How do you keep so cheerful no matter what?"

Francesca was staring at her classmate. They had both just learned that they had to repeat their grade. They had worked hard this year, but not enough to meet their high school requirements.

"It's not that easy, Francesca," Chiara said with a sigh, suddenly more serious. "To be honest, I miss Sassello. That's the little village where I grew up, you know. Here, we're in the big city."

"Someone told me your faith in God is very strong. Is that true?" Francesca asked. "You never talk about it."

"The important thing isn't talking about faith. What's important is living it, right?"

After a pause, Chiara added, with sparkles in her eyes: "But yeah, if I have a secret that keeps me cheerful, that's the one!"

A Brutal Diagnosis

"Ow!"

The other tennis players looked at Chiara, who had dropped her racket on the court, groaning and wincing in pain. The game was stopped, and everyone rushed to her.

"What's wrong?"

"I must have dislocated my shoulder," she said. "It's nothing."

She has already regained her smile despite the nagging pain.

"Just keep playing. It will go away."

The match resumed. Then Chiara went back home to lie down. It was hurting so badly!

All through the fall, her shoulder caused her intense pain, but the doctors didn't know the reason. At the beginning of 1989, more extensive tests revealed that she was suffering from an advanced bone cancer.

Chiara was shaken. Her parents were devastated. But their shared faith helped them to face the ordeal together. All pain finds a meaning if offered to God, and Chiara was certain this was true. She would hold on to her faith until the end.

Panel 1:
— Hi, Chiara! How are you feeling today?
— Better! I was even able to make some bracelets.

Panel 2:
— You are so strong.
— This mission in Benin needs our help.

Chiara got involved in a project to help children in Benin, West Africa.

Panel 3:
— Everything falls into place when we offer it to Jesus.

Chiara is often the one who comforts her visitors.

Panel 4:
1990. She is getting worse but is still in high spirits and takes Communion every day.

Panel 5:
— Mama, could you read again the sentence with the six S's?
— Sarò santa se sono santa subito.*

*I will be a saint if I'm holy right now.

Panel 6:
— Are you in pain?
— Yeah, I'm carrying the cross with Jesus.

Chiara decided to dedicate her suffering to the world, in such need of God.

Panel 7:
— Do you like it, Chiara?
— Yes, that's the one I want.
— When you dress me, remember that I'm seeing Jesus.

Chiara prepares for her funeral the way others prepare for a party.

Panel 8:
— Ciao Mama. Be happy, because I am.

October 7, 1990. These were the last words of Chiara on the day of her death.

Panel 9:
— This luminous girl is a model for young people, and for all of us.

Chiara was beatified on September 25, 2010, by Pope Benedict XVI.

CHIARETTA, a Light for the World

Surname: Badano
First name: Chiara (nicknames: Chiaretta and Chiara Luce)
Born: October 29, 1971, in Sassello, Italy
Died: October 7, 1990, in Sassello, Italy
Parents: Ruggero Badano and Maria Teresa Badano
Moments of weakness: Struggled with her trust in God at times in the last months: "How hard it is to live out Christianity all the way to the end!"
Moments of strength: Keeping her joy throughout her illness
Patroness of: Athletes

Did You Know?

Chiara and Benin
While bedridden, Chiara generously sponsored the project of an Italian engineer who founded a mission in Benin, Africa, to help children there. She donated all her savings to support it and took advantage of every little break from her pain to make small items that could be sold for the benefit of the mission.

TESTIMONIAL FROM A FRIEND OF CHIARA

"Visiting Chiaretta was like walking into an elevator. She would lift up the simplest things on earth to meet the beauty of heaven. And the things of heaven, so abstract and complicated for someone like me, who didn't believe, came down to earth to become simple. In her presence, you touched heaven and earth at the same time, and after you went back to the world, you were already looking forward to seeing her again."

Quote from Chiara
"Every moment is precious, so don't waste it. If we live it well, everything makes sense. Everything is relative—even the most awful moments—if we give it to Jesus. Pain is never wasted, but it makes sense as a gift to Jesus."

Timeline:

- **October 29, 1971:** Birth of Chiara Badano
- **1980:** Chiara joins the Focolare Movement.
- **1982:** Chiara enters middle school. She is a very good student.
- **1985:** Chiara repeats her first year of high school.
- **1988:** She starts to feel pain in her shoulder
- **February 1989:** Chiara is diagnosed with bone cancer.
- **June 18, 1990:** After all the hospital's treatments fail, Chiara returns to Sassello, her hometown.
- **October 7, 1990:** Death of Chiara
- **September 25, 2010:** Beatification of Chiara by Pope Benedict XVI

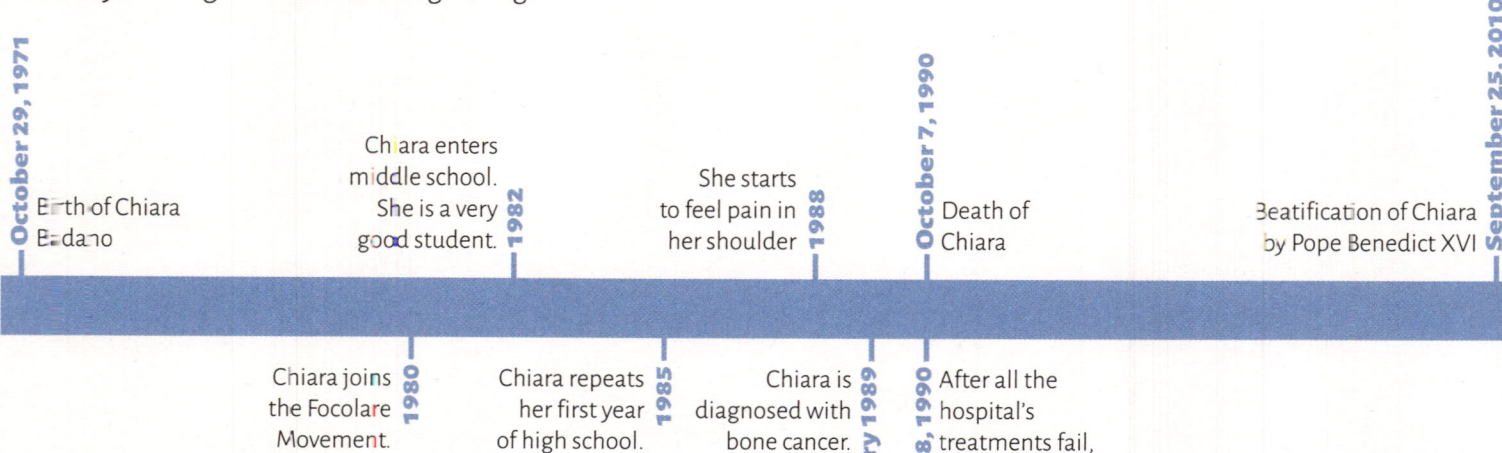

Prayer to Blessed Chiara Badano

Blessed Chiara Luce,
you knew how to let these words of Jesus resonate within you:
"You are the light of the world."
You never stopped allowing this light to grow within you,
never veiling it or letting it waver,
even when the test of illness could have darkened your life.

With affection we say your name,
and we ask for your help.
Help us, like you, to be the light of the world
through our joy for life and our love of God and neighbor.

Watch over those who are sick and the families who love them.
Pray for and comfort all who are going through hardship.
Help them, like you, to set their eyes on the joys of heaven,
which lessen and ease all the sufferings on earth.
Amen.

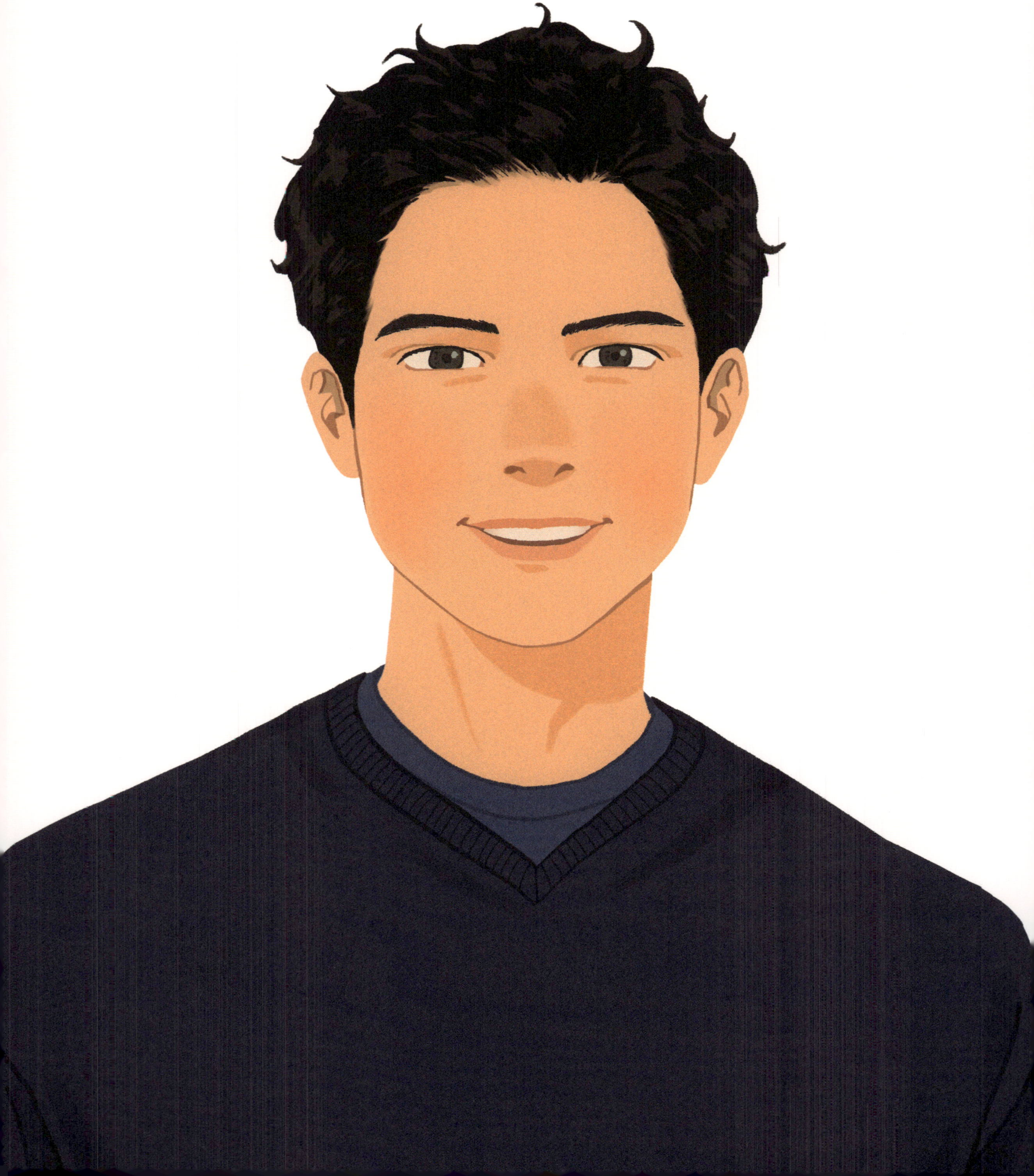

Blessed Carlo Acutis
(1991–2006)

Carlo Acutis was an active boy—happy, curious, and open-minded. He played saxophone and soccer. He wore sweatshirts and sneakers. Born just as the world was entering the Internet age, he became passionate about technology very young. In many ways, he was just an ordinary boy.

The Stadium and the Altar

Tonight, the San Siro stadium in Milan was full again, and the fans' cheers could be heard all over the city. In Italy, soccer always attracts great crowds. Meanwhile, a few miles from there, a teenager was praying in a church that was almost empty. Instead of a soccer ball, the boy was contemplating the white circle of a Eucharistic Host, in which he recognized Jesus, the Savior of the world. Carlo felt the loving presence of God close to him. Though Carlo loved soccer, he kept asking himself: "Why don't people line up here? They should come in bigger numbers than they do at the game!"

A Habit of Prayer

Carlo considered this question with his whole being. He loved life passionately and put at its center what he perceived as one essential: God.

Carlo was not born into a practicing Catholic family, but when he was four, his grandfather died of a heart attack and then appeared to him in a dream, asking for his help to enter heaven. From then on, the child began to pray with fervor. This habit never left him.

The Eucharist: Source of His Energy

At seven years old, Carlo received his First Communion. That day, he made himself a special promise: he would go to Mass every day of his life. He went to church every night after school. The joy and the energy he got from it shone all around him. His mother, his father, and their housekeeper, Rajesh, were the first to feel this light. His parents began to embrace his faith, and even Rajesh, of Hindu origin, converted to Christianity after hearing the little boy speak about Jesus with such simplicity and conviction.

God's Geek

Years went by. Active, fun-loving, simple, and funny, Carlo kept his faith alive and tried to make each day worthy of heaven. It was his daily objective, and he liked to repeat: "The Eucharist is my highway to heaven." Carlo volunteered to help the poor at a local soup kitchen run by the Capuchin Friars and the Missionaries of Charity. He was also involved in multiple projects to evangelize people, including an elaborate website dedicated to Eucharistic miracles. With his passion for technology, he was able to share his faith through the Internet.

A Sudden Departure to Heaven

In October 2006, at the age of fifteen, Carlo got sick. At first it seemed to be a flu, but in fact, it was a devastating disease: leukemia. Hospitalized right away, Carlo was still able to keep his promise, thanks to a priest who came to celebrate Mass at his side until the day of his death on October 12.

"To be always united with Jesus, that is the goal of my life," he had said when still healthy. Not only was Carlo able to achieve his goal, but because of him, many other people joined the adventure of faith. At his funeral Mass, his parents were amazed to see the large crowd that came to honor their son: hundreds of strangers, neighbors, friends, homeless people.

Carlo was beatified in 2020, after a miracle due to his intercession was recognized by the Church. In accord with his wishes, he was buried in Assisi, his favorite city. Today Carlo continues to touch the hearts of many through his story and example.

Panel 1:
Good night, Carlo!
Good night! See you tomorrow!

Panel 2:
Ciao! I have something for you.

Panel 3:
I thought you'd be able to use it.
Thanks, Carlo. You are an angel!

Panel 4:
Do you want to stay and talk a while?
I'd love to, but I have a ton of work. I'll see you tomorrow.

Panel 5:
A good Mass, Carlo?
Yes, Mama!

Panel 6:
I found that book you wanted at the Polytechnic Institute.
Great! Thanks.

Panel 7:
After dinner...

Panel 8:
Don't work too late!
I won't, I promise. I'm done with math. Just working on the Eucharistic miracles website.

Panel 9:
Eucharistic Miracles Exhibit

Carlo got sick just as he was finishing the last touches of this online exhibit. Today it is still shown across the world.

CARLO, a High-Speed Connection with Heaven

Surname: Acutis
First name: Carlo
Born: May 3, 1991, in London, England
Died: October 12, 2006, in Monza, Italy
Parents: Andrea Acutis and Antonia Salzano Acutis
Siblings: Michele and Francesca (twins born in 2010)
Favorite city: Assisi
Interests: Computers, music (saxophone), nature, animals
Moments of weakness: Put his health in danger by staying up late working
Moments of strength: Joy, a love of the Eucharist, courage in caring for others
Patron of: Computer programmers and youth

☞ **HIS LAST WORDS:** "I'm glad to die because I lived my life without wasting a single minute on doing things that do not please God."

☞ **CLOSE TO SAINT FRANCIS** Carlo spent his holidays in Assisi, the city of Saint Francis, where his family had a house. He loved this town, with its many churches, still alive with the story of the Little Poor Man. Faith, generosity, simplicity, unlimited trust in God, affection for nature and animals: although almost eight hundred years apart, Carlo had a lot to share with Saint Francis! Carlo's body rests now in Assisi, in a chapel open to the public.

Did You Know?

Brazil, October 12, 2010. A little boy, Matheus, was at the center of his family's prayers. Born with a severe deformity of the pancreas, he couldn't eat normally. Four years to the day after Carlo was called to God, a parish priest who had read about the Italian teenager online suggested praying to him. Matheus came back home cured. His pancreas had healed, and he was able to eat normally. After a long investigation, this inexplicable healing was attributed to the intercession of Carlo Acutis and led to his beatification. Beyond this official case, his parents have received many other testimonies of miraculous healings.

Non Io, ma Dio
It was Carlo's motto, in a rhyming form. In Italian, it means, "Not me, but God."

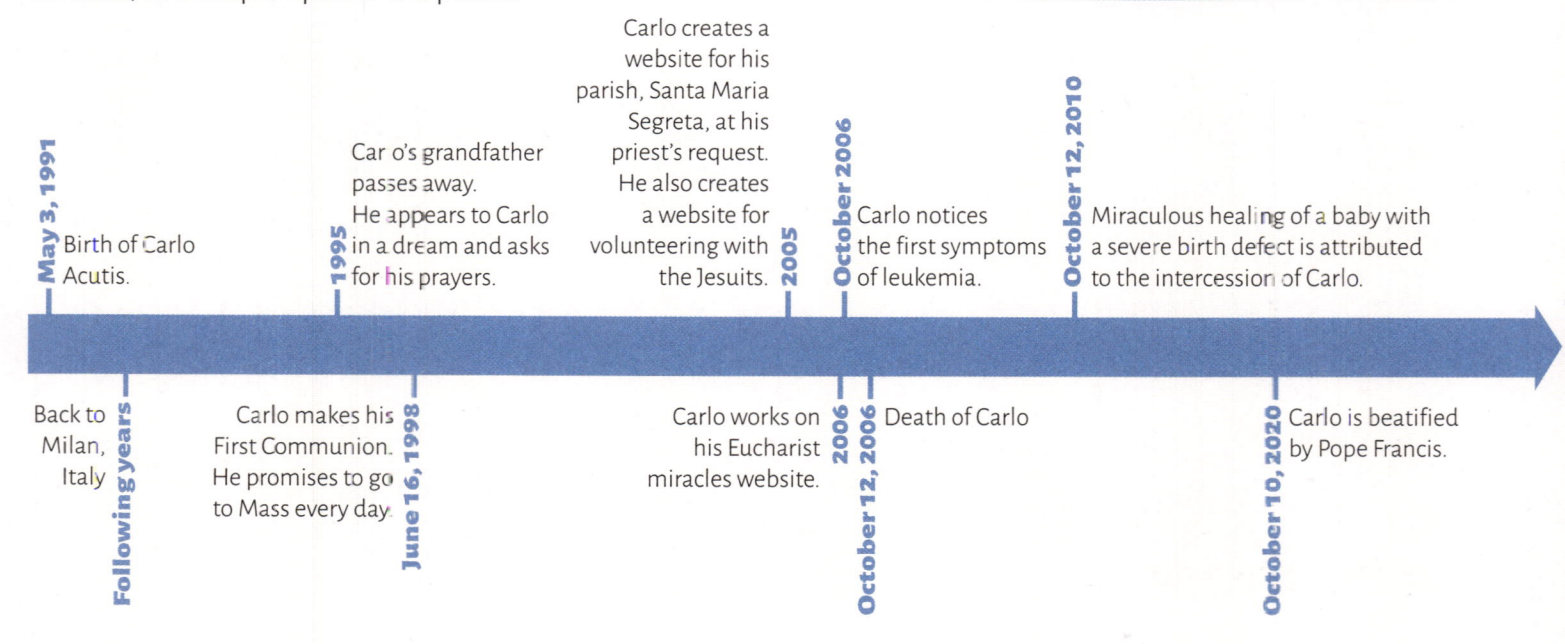

May 3, 1991 — Birth of Carlo Acutis.

Following years — Back to Milan, Italy

1995 — Carlo's grandfather passes away. He appears to Carlo in a dream and asks for his prayers.

June 16, 1998 — Carlo makes his First Communion. He promises to go to Mass every day.

2005 — Carlo creates a website for his parish, Santa Maria Segreta, at his priest's request. He also creates a website for volunteering with the Jesuits.

2006 — Carlo works on his Eucharist miracles website.

October 2006 — Carlo notices the first symptoms of leukemia.

October 12, 2006 — Death of Carlo

October 12, 2010 — Miraculous healing of a baby with a severe birth defect is attributed to the intercession of Carlo.

October 10, 2020 — Carlo is beatified by Pope Francis.

Prayer to Blessed Carlo Acutis

Blessed Carlos,
you whose heart burned before the Eucharist,
help us to recognize the presence of Jesus in the Host
and to welcome him with love.

You who cared about the poor,
inspire us with your generosity and your dedication to service.

You who defended the weakest,
help us to learn from your example
and treat those around us with kindness and respect.

You who were always cheerful,
help us to be happy in our hearts too.

You who used your talents and your smile
to announce Jesus and to share your faith,
pray that God will increase in us the desire to share with the world
the Word of God, which is the source of life.
Amen.

Printed by Dimograf, Poland, in May 2024.
Job number 24L0247
Printed in compliance with The Consumer Safety Act, 2008.